CONSCIOUSNESS
OF
BATTLE

OTHER BOOKS

The Theology of Romantic Love
A Creed for a Christian Skeptic

CONSCIOUSNESS
OF
BATTLE

An Interim Report
on a Theological Journey

by

MARY McDERMOTT SHIDELER

*To me also was given, if not Victory, yet the consciousness
of Battle, and the resolve to persevere therein while life
or faculty is left.*

THOMAS CARLYLE, *Sartor Resartus*

17003

WILLIAM B. EERDMANS PUBLISHING COMPANY
GRAND RAPIDS, MICHIGAN

Printed in the United States of America

In Loving Memory
of
KATHRYN BENBROOK LAPP

because she asked me the questions
which this book was written to answer,
and found her own answers before she died

Almighty God, we entrust all who are dear to us to Thy
never-failing care and love, for this life and the life to come,
knowing that Thou art doing for them better things than
we can desire or pray for, through Jesus Christ our Lord.
Amen.

TABLE OF CONTENTS

Prologue

7

Living Theologically

Epilogue

PROLOGUE

Five senses; an incurably abstract intellect; a haphazardly selective memory; a set of preconceptions and assumptions so numerous that I can never examine more than a minority of them — never become even conscious of them all. How much of total reality can such an apparatus let through?

C. S. LEWIS, *A Grief Observed*

chapter one

DO-IT-YOURSELF THEOLOGY

*The great doctrines are the only explanation and the only
hope. But even the great doctrines are only the statement
of something as wide as the universe and as deep as the
human heart.*

CHARLES WILLIAMS, "Natural Goodness"

This is an interim report on a theological journey which began
when I nearly committed suicide, and which I hope will continue
until I die. I have written it in order to explain what theology
is, how a theologian goes about his business, and why people
become theologians at all.

I had been working in theology for some years and had published a book and several articles in the field before discovering
belatedly how few of my friends and acquaintances had any clear
idea of how theologians operate and what they are trying to do.
Most other vocations, from housekeeping to nuclear physics, have
been described in scores of popular magazines and books, so that
most reasonably well informed persons have some notion of
what goes on in scientific laboratories, business offices, factories,
and farms. But by and large, the process of theologizing is as
mysterious to most laymen as if theologians had conspired to hide
their labors from the profane view of the uninitiated.

On the contrary, there is nothing intrinsically obscure about
theologizing, and the theologians I know best are eager, sometimes to the point of impatience, to share all their skills and
conclusions with anyone who will listen to them. Their explanations, however, often presuppose that their hearers already understand that theology is not so much a rational science or super-

natural revelation as a continuing activity of persons, and its methods are not so much those of instruction as of exploration. Since relatively few persons do have such a background, it is not surprising that theological books, articles, and sermons that are directed to laymen so frequently miss their mark, or that laymen so rarely see how theological discussion applies to their concerns and thus find it simply confusing.

A comment recently made by an acquaintance, and a question repeatedly asked of me by friends, have brought sharply home to me the discrepancy between the theologians' understanding of theology and that of many who are outside the field. After a meeting of university students where I was a resource leader, one of the men remarked, "You're a theologian, so of course you have to defend your church's position." And my conversations with friends on religious and theological matters have been thickly studded with their inquiry, "Where did you get that idea?" — for example, that despair is the natural state of man, or that Christian love is not an emotional state.

The student was making the common error of supposing that the primary function of theology is apologetic, in the limited sense that the foremost theological task is to state and defend ideas which the theologian has adopted on the blanket authority of some institution or tradition. It had never occurred to him that one might adhere to the institution or tradition because it represented beliefs which one had embraced for entirely different — and intellectually respectable — reasons. Nor did he realize what his remark implied about the intellectual, moral, and personal integrity of theologians. They are indeed devoted to vindicating as well as to discovering a faith, but normally their first loyalty is to the truth and not to an institution, tradition, or set of dogmas.

My friends' problem was more subtle. At first I understood their question, "Where did you get that idea?" to mean, "What was your source? Where did you come across it? Who originally formulated it?" — and I answered by referring to the history of Christian thought or my reading in related subjects, in order to demonstrate that the notion had reputable antecedents and was not my own invention. Such a response, however, was consistently unsatisfying to them. Even those who agreed with whatever proposition was under argument kept pressing me for another kind of answer. In time I learned that they were really asking,

"What makes that idea persuasive or significant for you?" They needed to know what in my own experience had convinced me of the truth or error of the position I was describing.

Most of these people were fairly naive theologically, but all of them were far too sophisticated to confuse personal witness with rational proof. At the stage when they asked that question, they were simply not interested in rational proofs for the eminently sound reason that they were intelligent enough to work those out for themselves when the time for it arrived, and they sensed that that time had not yet come. Their need was for something more fundamental: to comprehend how the theological issues were related to their own lives, and this they could grasp only when they saw how someone else's life was tied in with the formal statements and problems. It was futile to say to them, "The natural state of man is despair"; the abstract proposition did not belong to the same realm of discourse as their immediate anguish. My job, then, became to demonstrate in immediate, personal terms how theology grows out of experience and how experience is affected by theology. Because while theological statements are usually expressed objectively, the great doctrines in all religions are the products of passionate wrestling with the elemental powers of darkness, ignorance, pride, sloth, and despair — and of light, beauty, and joy. To know that theologians of the past confronted those powers is reassuring. But to see a contemporary actually engaged in the struggle is illuminating. We do not know our own hearts until another has revealed his to us. We cannot give our best to the battle when we think we are fighting only for — and by — ourselves.

In the first instance, theology is the attempt to make sense out of everything. Christian theology indeed starts with the person of Jesus called the Christ, but the Christian theologian may well travel a long road before he reaches that point of departure, and the premises on which he bases his Christian theology are rarely the products of an arbitrary choice or of unbroken allegiance to childhood loyalties. Those premises are far more likely to represent conclusions drawn from an extensive chain of previous reasoning and a long accumulation of experience. As a wedding marks the end of one phase in the participants' lives as well as the beginning of a new phase, so the adoption of Christianity marks the end of one pattern of thought and the beginning of another.

We begin to theologize whenever we try to understand the world we live in, and to find our place in that world. All of us play around with theological questions and ideas in the ordinary course of living. The theologian works with them. What the rest of us do casually and incidentally, he does deliberately and with educated care. And where we are likely to be satisfied with an understanding of life that meets our temporary requirements, he seeks for an understanding that will fulfil the requirements of many persons at many times — ideally, of all men in all times and places.

Once that activity belonged to the domain of philosophy, and it may again, but for some years philosophers have tended to limit their professional attention to the analysis of language and the processes of reasoning. Subsequently, the orphaned problems have found a home in certain parts of the theological community, so that today the discipline of theology is widely interpreted as including the great questions about the nature of the world and of man, many of the great problems of knowledge, and above all, the synthesis that is still referred to as "a philosophy of life", whether it affirms or denies any kind of God, or ignores the idea of God entirely.

This book constitutes an attempt to describe how theologies grow out of the interplay between experience and reflection. My purpose is partly to fill a gap in general knowledge, and partly to give laymen a background from which they can go into further study of theology. But principally, I want to show how any thoughtful and resolute person can develop and clarify his own theology — a purpose which is so important to me that I was tempted to entitle the book, *How to Become a Theologian in Eight Easy Lessons,* instead of giving it the formal and rather pretentious name that it bears.

Like writers of do-it-yourself books in other areas, I faced at the outset three possible approaches to the subject: "This is how it ought to be done"; "This is how somebody (presumably an expert) does it"; and "This is how I did it". I could be pontifical, biographical, or confidential.

The pontifical style has a comfortingly authoritative ring. It makes the reader feel safe by giving him the impression that there is one right way to proceed, and that if he follows the designated steps in the assigned order, he will accomplish what he set out to do. However, it discourages the reader from handling his material imaginatively, and is apt to be excruciatingly dull to read.

The writer who chooses the biographical or the confidential approach may avoid the slough of tedium only to fall into the pit of idiosyncrasy. He may stress his subject's peculiarities until others cannot see any connection between those problems, methods, and conclusions, and their own. On the other hand, the more personal styles of presentation invite the reader to share in the processes of questioning and discovering, and thereby encourage him to exercise his own imagination and initiative.

In my case, the choice of the confidential style appeared to have not only that advantage, but also three others. First, the simplicities of a layman's theologizing might serve as a better introduction for other laymen than the exquisite complexities of a professional's. Second, because I am a layman, no one would be in serious danger of taking my conclusions as authoritative or of overlooking the methods by which they were reached. Third, there would be no need to speculate about the direct influences that contributed to my theological development, because I know more details about myself than I could possibly learn about anyone else.

Let it be understood at once, however, that while I claim to know myself in more detail than I could know any other person, "more detail" does not imply impeccable accuracy. No doubt some of my theologizing reflects rationalization, self-deception, and wishful or fearful thinking, rather than clear observation and sound reasoning. I cannot entirely trust my analysis of my motives or my memory of straightforward events, not to mention the completeness of my journals. Self-knowledge is the end, not the beginning, of wisdom, and I do not pretend to have achieved it. But I need have no hesitation about asserting that specific incidents, such as my father's death, affected my theology in certain ways. I do not need to speculate on its place in the growth of my theology, as I would have to in the case of another theologian.

Here I have been as honest and as accurate as I could be. If the self I portray is partly fictional, it is not because I wanted or intended to display anything more or other than what happened. Facing the inescapable inaccuracies, I comfort myself with the reminder that my purpose is to illustrate a process, a method, an approach, and that as long as the illustration clarifies the point to which it is directed, it matters little if at all whether the illustration comes from fiction or non-fiction. In the end, the process could be exhibited just as well by a novelist using imaginary characters and fabricated events, and I would have done it that way if I could have.

However, writing a book like this is as much a method of discovery as a report on what has already been discovered. Therefore time after time I have rewritten or replaced entire sections, either because my mind changed while I was working on them, or because once they were on paper where I could look at them, I realized that I had not thought out the problems as thoroughly as I should have. On other occasions, I have allowed ideas to stand as they were originally formulated, even though I have since gone beyond them or in a quite different direction. If my intention were to exhibit a finished product or a perfected technique, such adaptations and retentions would be indefensible. Since it is instead to depict a procedure that is still going on, the point where I stop revising is necessarily determined not by the finality of my conclusions, but by a decision that is more influenced by considerations of structure and style than by logic.

In order to exhibit the continuity of my theological development — that it was not entirely haphazard or arbitrary — I have not only abbreviated and simplified the narrative in the first part of the book, but have also omitted certain matters that could not be brought within that framework. Although my struggles with those issues contributed substantially to the building of the pattern that is sketched under "Creating a Theology," I can rarely identify the sequence in which I worked on them, or recall how long it took to work through them. Neither can I determine in most of those cases whether the solutions resulted from prior theological clarifications, or whether clarity emerged during my labors with them. Therefore I have arranged the material in the second part, "Living Theologically," by grouping related problems rather than by following a temporal order.

Occasionally, a problem that was discussed in an early chapter will reappear in a later one. Such returns — they are not duplications — are deliberate. Theological issues are almost never solved once and for all. They recur in new guises or at new levels of urgency and penetration. Simplicities open upon complexities, and complexities resolve themselves into simplicities, compelling us to re-evaluate both their original forms and their later expressions. Or we throw a devil out of the window, and he creeps back in through a crack in the floor.

For the benefit of readers like myself, who find it helpful to have a chronological frame of reference for a narrative, I have placed an autobiographical summary and a list of dates at the conclusion of this prologue. Otherwise, historical sequence has been followed only where it concurs with my conscious theological growth. My frequent use of the flashback technique is not merely a literary trick. Often in the history of my thought, the theological significance of an event became apparent only many years after its occurrence, and I have decided that the connection between such incidents and the mainstream of my theological development will be more readily grasped if they are introduced at the point where they enter that stream instead of in their chronological position.

Autobiographical Summary

I was born and brought up in Topeka, Kansas, the second child of a lawyer who later became a judge of the United States Circuit Court of Appeals, and of his very young and beautiful wife. My sister was a year and a half older than I, my brother four years younger. I attended the Topeka public schools, and entered Swarthmore College when I was 17. There I majored in psychology, and minored in philosophy and zoology. My father died suddenly of pneumonia during my junior year. Following graduation, I spent a year at home with my mother and sister, my brother then being away at college. The fall of 1939, I entered Chicago Theological Seminary to study the psychology of religion. Almost immediately, I fell in love with both theology and a theological student. My husband and I were married at the end of my first year in seminary, which was his last. After three pastorates, he finished his doctoral work in historical theology at the Divinity School of the University of Chicago; since 1947, he has been engaged in college and university teaching of philosophy and religion. We have no children. I have been writing seriously and steadily since 1955.

List of Dates

Year	My age	Event
1917		birth
1919	2	unanswerable question about the house

1923?	6?	question whether I believed in fairies
1926	9?	my first pair of glasses
1932	15	confirmed in the Episcopal Church
1933	16	the dream
1934	16	appendectomy
1934	17	entered Swarthmore College
1935	18	"Why live?"
1937	19	death of my father
1938	20	graduated from college
1939	22	entered Chicago Theological Seminary
1940	22	married; joined the Society of Friends
1945	27	death of my brother
1946	29	entered Pendle Hill
1949	32	first heard of Charles Williams
1960	42	my book on Charles Williams accepted for publication; began *A Creed for a Christian Skeptic*
1962	44	began the first draft of this book
1963	45	25th reunion of my college class
1963	46	reinstated in the Episcopal Church
1968	50	*A Creed for a Christian Skeptic* published
1968	51	finished this book

CREATING A THEOLOGY

He said not: "Thou shalt not be tempested, thou shalt not be travailed, thou shalt not be dis-eased"; but he said: "Thou shalt not be overcome."

JULIAN OF NORWICH, *Revelations of Divine Love*

chapter two

The Jumping-Off Place

"...How is one to know which things are really of over-mastering importance?"
"We can only know that...when they have overmastered us."

DOROTHY L. SAYERS, *Gaudy Night*

1. *An Existential Question*

I was eighteen and a sophomore in college when the question, "Why live?" became so pressing that I could not continue living without an answer to it. The alternative, which I was actively considering, was suicide. I had come to a jumping-off place.

Questions like this do not originate spontaneously, although they may arise for reasons which a scientifically detached observer would judge to be foolish. The previous year I had fallen head-long and hopelessly in love with another student who had no interest in me at all. In my journal I called him "the Little Tin God": it was a significant title. Strictly speaking I worshipped him, despite my clear knowledge that no human being could deserve such adoration. The fire in my heart did not quite consume my intellect or my sense of my absurdity, but I could not quench the flames with rational argument or self-ridicule, and I did not know of any other extinguishers.

Despairing love, however, constituted only part of the background for my question. I was also at odds with my family, and had been ever since I could remember. We were separated by mutual misunderstandings, and were mutually antagonized by differences in interest, conviction, and temperament. I grated on them and they on me, a situation so common that to spell out its details would be pointless.

My parents had done everything possible to encourage the development of their children into useful citizens who would be a satisfaction to themselves and others, and my sister and brother grew gracefully under that regimen. I was also growing, but not gracefully or graciously. I was — or saw myself as being — irremediably homely and awkward, socially inept, intellectually mediocre, emotionally confused, and in general thoroughly unlovable: a messy assemblage of qualities that cancelled each other out or created frightful discords. Hitherto my family had found me exceptionally difficult to live with, and in all likelihood they would need to invest an appalling amount of further concern, effort, and money in me before they or society would receive even the scantiest return. Would I ever be worth their struggle, not to mention my own? Would it not be better for them if I cut their losses, giving them the short grief at my death and the long relief of my absence?

On the other hand, I had experienced moments of ecstasy, and the hope of their return was almost enough to make any life worth living. I was blessed or cursed with a driving curiosity, and there were a thousand things I wanted to find out and do before I died. It seemed a shame to waste my parents' contribution to me since conceivably I might sometime be useful to somebody. Were the occasional raptures worth the deadly seasons between? Is life worth living? When is life worth living? When is suicide justifiable?

Theologians call this an existential question because it involves the whole existence of the person asking it. Existential questions are not limited to the decision for or against suicide; they may equally well refer to a choice between alternative ways of living. But characteristically, they are disturbing enough to the questioner that his actions as well as his ideas are at stake, and the answer he reaches will directly influence not only his theories about life and other abstract ideas, but also his day-by-day and hour-by-hour behavior.

In its broadest theological meaning, existentialism refers to a general type of problem and a method for its solution. In a narrower sense, it specifies various solutions. Here I shall use the term only in its widest meaning, as representing the conviction that the basic problems for man are those which embrace his entire life, rather than those which are primarily rational or practical. I am not prepared to assert categorically that all theologies have their source in existential problems. My impression is that they do, although in some instances the existential reference is so deeply hidden that it is difficult to identify.

Since professional theologians do not always agree on what theology is, it would be impertinent for me to define it except in a very general way, by saying that here I shall be concerned with theology only so far as it is existential, not with the enterprise regarded as the defense of a system of received dogmas, or the completion of a jigsaw puzzle whose pieces are biblical texts, or an exhibition of skill in manipulating abstractions, or as the construction of a decorative artifact.

Inevitably — and properly — the professional theologian climbs from the foothills into the high mountains, from the comparatively low levels where I am trying to coordinate thought and action, to the lofty altitudes where scholars investigate precise implications and survey tremendous vistas. Thus every "answer" that I have reached will raise for the professional a multitude of technical questions, some of which I already see but am not ready or not able to debate in their terms, and many which I cannot even see the point of. They work at elevations where I cannot breathe, yet they began their theological activity on the plains of infancy, childhood, and adolescence like all the rest of us, and learned on hillocks like our own the rudiments of climbing.

Every theologian has his own jumping-off place, a particular question or situation that he feels impelled to resolve. "Where can I find something that I can really trust?" "Why did this have to happen to me?" "Why should I bother?" "How can I explain — or endure — such evils?" "Who am I?" These belong in the same category with my "Why live?" as direct responses to unbearable tensions.

Another category comprises questions arising from the conflict of two or more incompatible ideas, and hence incompatible ways of life. Thomas Aquinas could not bear to abandon the teachings either of Christianity or of Aristotelian philosophy, yet they appeared to be irreconcilable. In trying to bring them into harmony, he produced one of the most magnificent structures of thought in history. The conflict of science with religion belongs to this group, as do the battles of church against state, of individual conscience against social pressures, of dogma against dogma.

Still another category of existential questions can be illustrated by my mentor, Charles Williams, who discovered with delight the affinity between romantic love and Christianity, and set himself to explore their relationships in detail. This class contains relatively few members, most of whom — unlike Williams — are mystics, so that it would scarcely be worth mentioning were it not that it corrects the widespread identification of existentialism with despair, horror, fragmentation, and meaninglessness. Yet our pleasures move us as often and as profoundly as our troubles do. The problem of joy is no less immediate than the problems of evil and pain. The existential shock of falling in love is as overwhelming, and theologically as significant, as the existential shock of dread, and is probably much more common.

In studying any theology, one of the first things to look for is the living issue that lies beneath the abstract phrases and neatly organized systems. What is the theologian worried or exalted by? What is he fighting against and for? My own investigations lead me to suggest that the principal opponent of most theologians is meaninglessness: the fear that no life has any ultimate purpose and no effort any permanent significance.

The Gorgon of unmeaning can reveal herself in many guises: the terror of death or judgment, the sense of futility, the abhorrence of ugliness or irrationality or depravity, a generalized anxiety or disgust, and an indefinite number of others. A few theologians make clear what specific form their enemy takes, and describe the personal details of their meeting and joining battle — Augustine of Hippo and Søren Kierkegaard come at once to mind. But not all theologians have the inclination for such candor or appreciate its value for the theological enterprise, and those who do adopt that manner of presentation become vulnerable to the impertinent attentions of Peeping Toms, gossips, and dilettantes in psychoanalysis. But though the personal form of communication can be a form of spiritual strip-tease or an exercise in emotional catharsis, it is sometimes the only method for getting a point across to persons who are in grave need of just this sort of illumination.

The relation of personal confession to theological doctrine is itself a theological problem. In an extremely important sense, biography and autobiography have nothing to do with theology because a theology, as a pattern of understanding, must be judged on its merits as a pattern. In an equally important sense, however, personal experience and theology are inseparable. The teachings of religious leaders and the official dogmas of religious bodies are not meant as solutions to equations in formal logic. They were and are developed in response to living problems of living persons, and when cut away from that personal reference, they lose their vitality, their meaning, and their significance. We need "pure" theology as we need "pure" science, but even the purest of scientific investigations derives its impetus from a very human curiosity, and the scientist is not satisfied with his ruminations until he has tested them by laboratory experiments or meticulous observations of natural phenomena. No aspect of science, much less of theology, can be completely divorced from the human beings who engage in it, and since theology is expressly concerned with the nature of man, the lives of individual men have direct bearing on the origin and application of theological concepts.

Because every theologian is a unique person, his theology is inescapably limited by his individuality. But he is also a representative of mankind, sharing its common life. Being a part of the universe he is trying to comprehend, his own perceptions and responses are as likely as anything else to be generally instructive. Conversely, anything else is as likely to be illuminating as his private or exceptional experiences. His fundamental concern, however, is not to express his exclusive self. He is inclusively concerned with general principles and insights that are widely applicable to the genus *homo* to which he belongs, and the world in which *homo* lives. His work is intended not solely as a commentary upon himself, but as a commentary upon the life of which he is a part, so he usually writes in general terms about general problems lest his readers become so engrossed in the illustration that they lose sight of his theme and the exposition fail of its purpose. So doing, however, he leaves to his reader the delicate and complicated task of discovering how those general propositions are related to actual living, which is where the theological enterprise comes to life.

2. *A Psychological Question*

"Why live?" I marshalled my reasons for and against living as if the question were an intellectual one, although nearly all sophisticated observers, then and now, would challenge that diagnosis. Surely I was suffering from a severe emotional disturbance and needed psychotherapy rather than rational disputation. Surely my chronic emotional instability had blown up into an acute emotional storm — and it seemed obvious that psychological turmoils cannot be quieted with arguments, any more than intellectual problems (for instance, in mathematics or mechanics) can be solved by psychotherapy. Surely the plain need was to treat my emotional difficulties, and when they were taken care of, the intellectual issues would evaporate or I could deal with them in an appropriately detached fashion at my leisure. In short, the doctrine of man that prevailed when and where I was living stipulated the division of my question into two co-ordinate questions, of which the more pressing was psychological, to be handled personally but irrationally, and the more comprehensive was philosophical, to be treated rationally but impersonally.

I could not accept that diagnosis, As a child in grade school, I had discovered that intellectual problems can have piercing emotional effects, and that some emotional problems can be solved by rational, if indirect, methods. I remember a tantrum when I could not work an arithmetic assignment, and how swiftly my frenzy dissipated when someone showed me where I had misunderstood the teacher's directions. My reason and my emotions functioned together; together they acted upon and were affected by my body. The separation of my question, "Why live?" into psychological and philosophical parts implied a separation in me for which I could find no evidence. I was one person; the question was also one.

My reaction against the division of reason from emotion was the more vehement because I intuitively felt that philosophy and psychology ought to be congenial companions, but the Gestalt psychology I studied in one class had no discernible connection with the rationalist philosophy expounded in another, and in both cases, such agonizing perplexities as mine lay outside the scope of lectures and class discussions. Students and professors were immersed in the vital questions of What, Where, When, How, and Who; nobody except myself appeared to be asking Why on the level where I was engaged.

Looking back, I am sure that I must have been abominably imperceptive or that my memory is gravely at fault. It is extremely improbable that my associates cared as little about the meaning of life as their genial appearance led me to suppose. But however deluded I may have been, I sensed here another form of the dichotomy between rational thought and the richness of living. And because the people around me seemed so serene and secure, I tried to closet my terrifying uncertainties. To some degree, of course, I failed. The criticism, "You're too intense," was flung at me more times than I can count, each time puzzling and wounding me more deeply. What the closet held might not be visible, but that it contained something was embarrassingly plain.

As if this were not enough, the popular interpreters of Freud had found in me a ready disciple. I was sure that my unconscious was a cesspool, and it was obvious that my conscious motives and purposes were a dreary mixture of virtue and depravity. The fact that everyone else was presumably in the same situation provided no consolation: if no one else were any better off, there was no one to whom I could turn for help. Still further, I was oppressed by the awareness that most of my associates, at home as well as at school, had gifts and accomplishments that were greater than or different from my own, and my ungrudging admiration for them diminished my opinion of myself. Although I was not so infected with self-abasement as to take no credit for any brains or skills or good intentions, I was achingly aware of their defects and limitations. If I were the master of my fate, it was in exceedingly poor hands. Most certainly I was not the captain of my soul, but the slave of my disordered impulses. Moreover, the official pilots were essentially as unreliable as myself. They might be superior to me, but since they were not infallible, their authority over me must be limited. The situation was intolerable, and I could see no way out of it except death. Yet suicide in the absence of a positive reason was tantamount to evading the problem, and evasion was an indignity, a corruption, infinitely worse than failure.

The theological name for my condition during that period is despair. The attack was sharper than some persons endure, and longer in duration, but it was ludicrously typical. I was not going to go on living without a good reason, but I was not going to commit suicide without a good reason, either. I realized that even if I were to discover in complete detail exactly what psychological drives and aberrations had led me to ask my question, the question itself would not be answered, so that psychotherapy alone would be useless. But when I asked my question of philosophers in correctly impersonal terms, their impersonal replies left me more dissatisfied than ever. My courses in zoology had nothing helpful to offer: since it was natural for living things to try to keep on living, I must be unnatural for wanting not to live. Thus I felt guilty of a kind of blasphemy against life, as well as guilty for caring about something my contemporaries seemed not to be interested in, and guilty for my fear and confusion, and for my inability to master my guilt and fear.

Despair is common among men, although I did not know it then. According to Christian theology, it is the natural state of natural man — that is, of man before he has found his right relation to the world. It is rooted, obviously or obscurely, in man's recognition of his inability to deal satisfactorily with the world he confronts, or to answer all his own questions adequately, or to act in harmony with his surroundings in all circumstances, or to live as joyously and as nobly as he would like to, or even to adjust himself happily to his inadequacies.

The theological conclusions drawn from the experience of despair can be divided into two main groups: first, the assertion that it is an emotional state in which perceptions are blurred and perspectives displaced, so that one need not take seriously the picture of life which is seen by the person in despair; and second, the assertion that here a veil is lifted so that when we are in despair, we see life as it actually is.

The first of these positions implies a separation of intellect and emotion: the head repudiates the testimony of the heart. When the heart cries, "All is vanity!" or "The evil that I would not, that I do," the head replies, "Don't be silly. We're all frustrated, more or less. You're just fighting reality like a baby, or else you're inexcusably conceited, expecting yourself to be perfect. Anyway, just look at all that man has accomplished in spite of his weaknesses and flaws. Be reasonable. Be realistic. Despair is only a mood and it will pass. Meanwhile, go on with your work."

The advice to work is excellent. It is the best and perhaps the only way to keep the pain of despair at a level we can endure while we make our way through it. The description of despair as a mood is sound: it is certainly that. And the achievements of man, with all his limitations and defects, are vast beyond belief. But even if we grant the truth of those observations, they do not demonstrate that the world view of the despairing person is false. A mountain of meaningless accomplishments does not generate a meaning. The universality of imperfection does not make one's own imperfections more tolerable. The emotion of despair can result from a rationally justifiable conclusion: despair can be a theological position as well as an emotional state. The dispute between the despairing heart and the sanguine brain cannot be settled by summarily throwing out of court the evidence that conflicts with rationality, because the issue hinges upon the authority of the rational mind. Does it have the right to ignore or to suppress the perceptions and conclusions of the irrational — but not necessarily unreasonable — heart?

Some theologians assign such authority to the intellect. They admit into their discourse only ideas that can be defined clearly and distinctly, and defended on rigorously logical grounds. Conforming strictly to the laws of rational argument, they know nothing of Pascal's reasons of the heart, which belong to an order different from the austere arguments of the detached intellect. Other theologians take the opposite stand, bestowing full sovereignty upon the vision received in the experience of despair. Their position is most strikingly exhibited by the contemporary philosophers and artists who identify the real with the sordid, and the playwrights who have created the Theater of the Absurd. With tragic gallantry, they proclaim a gospel of meaninglessness to a world whose end they foresee as not the rapture of meaning made tangible and visible, or even the dignity of silence, but the obscenely senseless gabble of idiots.

All theologies must take account of despair. Many, like mine, begin with it. At that time, of course, I did not think that it was a beginning of anything. It felt more like the end of everything, as notes in my journal indicate. I wrote of "my great consolation in life: that I've got to die sometime." I remarked bitterly, "When one can see no reason for fighting, one is not much inclined to fight. . . . Hell, so what?" And again, "Only an integrated person can keep going in a mess — and I'm going to be integrated if I die trying." The passionate desire for integration required me to include both my intellect and my emotions, and both my ecstasies and despair, in the pattern of meaning I was trying to discover or create. But I could not see how they could possibly be associated without contaminating either the immaculate severity of the intellect or the sparkling honesty of my spontaneous emotions.

3. *The Outrage*

Such was my condition early in my sophomore year at college when I took my question, "Why live?" to Dr. Robert B. MacLeod, chairman of the psychology department and leader of an extracurricular seminar on the teachings of Jesus which a friend had persuaded me to join. Dr. MacLeod first satisfied himself that I was not on the verge of a psychotic break; then he proceeded to treat the question as a legitimate and important inquiry, and me as a reasonable and responsible person.

I had not known what to expect from Dr. MacLeod, but it was certainly not this. I was astonished to hear his assurance that my problem was not the fatuous quibbling of a dolt or neurotic but evidence of intellectual and personal competence. I was amazed when he told me that my despair resulted not from mental aberration but from pride, and that I was not tearing myself to pieces over a triviality or dreaming of an impossible consummation. I rejoiced to learn that there were methods for answering the question and for achieving the integration I sought. True, he consistently and wisely refused to tell me, at that time or any other, what he thought the answer was, or to list alternative possibilities, or to specify what methods I should use. But by being the person he was, he convinced me that an answer existed, and by his bearing toward me, he persuaded me that I could find it.

Dr. MacLeod found me hungering and thirsting for something I could not define and could scarcely imagine, and tormented by the fear that the universe contained nothing that would satisfy those cravings. By quieting my fear, he freed me to work at the problem of finding out what the universe did and did not contain, and what I was and was not capable of doing. The effect of that conference was not to generate an immediate transformation. My emotional storms did not abate overnight or for many years. I did not receive any significant new insights into the techniques or standards I might use in pursuing an answer to my question. My journal was still full of the Little Tin God, of my embarrassing efforts to write (and therefore to think and feel) with a "modern" sophistication about sex and other matters that are even more intimate, and of my ingenuous observations on Life. The same swampy ground quivered under my feet and the same miasma swirled around my head. Only now I had one fixed marker, like a stake driven through the mire to the rock beneath. Henceforth I could evaluate persons, ideas, and events in terms of their relevance to the central question, "Why live?" The question as such was solid. In a way, it was trustworthy. It gave me a stable point of reference which I hoped would enable me someday to find a stable frame of reference.

Once I had had such a frame of reference, a pattern of expectations, a set of standards, a world view, by which I could measure what was true or false, good or evil, sane or insane, healthy or sick. Its outlines are now almost impossible to recover because they were never consciously stated. Probably all children have similar proto-theologies: presumptions that the world will always be what they have known it to be. Thus a child who has always lived in the same place may respond to a move as if his world had come to an end — and in real sense, it has. Conversely, one who is used to frequent changes of place may discover a new world when he settles down for a long period. The child who has never been loved may not recognize or believe in love when he is given it; one who has consistently been loved may be incredulous of hate.

These frameworks cannot be carried intact from childhood into maturity. They are built out of experiences which are severely limited by the child's capacity to absorb, differentiate, and interpret, and when his later experience supplies him not with more building blocks but with new kinds of material — concrete instead of a sand pile, natural consequences instead of peremptory rewards and punishments — he must either reject the new materials or learn to build new kinds of structures. As I very well knew, my despair and my question had in great part resulted from the sudden disintegration of my childhood frame of reference, a few months before I entered college.

While I was in high school, I had been bothered by what was finally diagnosed as chronic appendicitis. Those were the days before antibiotics and plane travel, and my parents were reluctant to send me to a college half a continent away from them with an appendix that might at any time become acutely inflamed. So when I was admitted to the hospital for surgery, a couple of days after my graduation from high school, I was in excellent physical health and confident state of mind. None of us had any reason to suppose that the episode would have any significance other than as a brief interruption of my normal summer activities.

The night before the operation, however, without warning, my whole world went to pieces. I lay on the hospital bed flooded with waves of outrage. My body was about to be violated and, to compound the horror, I was consenting to that violation. This was not fear. To succumb to terror is not the same as to suffer an outrage. The prospect of the incision did not horrify me because it was a threat to my life or much of a threat to my comfort, but because it was an insult to the integrity of my body and therefore to my personal integrity.

So shattering was this sense of outrage that in the one operation, I lost both my vermiform appendix and the religion of my childhood. I woke from the anaesthetic to a world without meaning, where God no longer existed, where morality was nothing more than local custom, and where nothing in the entire universe could be trusted. Grimly — and only an adolescent can be quite so grim — I resolved never again to ground my life upon anything that would desert me as God and all that the name "God" implied had deserted me then. I would believe in nothing until I had tested it myself and proved it to be absolutely dependable.

During the next three months, the familiarity of the persons and places around me, and the comforting bonds of habit, gave me an illusion of continuing security. Then those structures also failed. At college, an immense range of new ideas and experiences burst upon me so swiftly and emphatically that I was stunned by its glory. I was dazzled by the autumn colors of the Pennsylvania countryside, by the incredible variety of possibilities laid out for my consideration in lectures and conversations, by trips to Philadelphia and walks alone in Crum woods. Here was a world in which anything might happen and I might become anyone. I plunged wildly into it (later Dr. MacLeod was to remark, "It's fun watching you grow, you do it so thoroughly") — and came perilously close to destruction.

The worst of my situation stemmed from the fact that after the breakdown of so many securities, I could not be sure whether any of those which were left would remain secure. I distrusted even those parts of my old frame of reference that had shown no signs of betraying me. "I don't know which side is up," I lamented regularly. I might just as well have said, "I don't know what is and isn't important," or "I don't know what to expect from life or myself," or "I don't know who I am." In such a period of transition, the two most immediate dangers are that one will lose hold of all structure and become demented, or that he will snatch at the first thing promising him stability and become set in a pitifully inadequate mold. Such crises are not the only spawning grounds for mental disease and fanaticism, but they are among the most fertile, and in so far as I have avoided either eventuality, the credit belongs to Dr. MacLeod.

The primary need for anyone who has lost his frame of reference is to discover something that he can hang onto, some belief or authority or standard of judgment or moral law or even question which is sufficiently stable that he can trust it to bear his weight. His primary difficulty is to test the supports he is offered. It is all very well to point out that his parents and mentors have found this or that fully adequate for their needs. He cannot be sure of its adequacy for him until he has tried it out for himself.

Not all people go through this type of crisis, and of those who do, not all undertake the testing procedure that consists of applying pressures to the object under examination to see how much it will endure before it shatters, and what the consequences of its shattering will be. We readily grant the appropriateness of such methods in many areas: we expect highway engineers to test their materials by breaking them down in order to ensure a generous margin of safety for travellers. We tend to be less happy about testing — or watching others test — the strength of moral and intellectual standards by deliberately breaking them. Thus a child will sometimes attack his parents to find out if he can really depend upon their love no matter what he does, and later he may break the rules they have laid down for him in order to determine for himself whether honesty really is the best policy or whether sexual experimentation actually does lead to grief. The principle behind the method is sound: only that which successfully resists us can be depended upon to support us. But to practise the principle in the way that I chose to is hazardous.

Any frame of reference (world view, principle, theology) especially needs testing for its rigidity and its flexibility. Before the appendectomy, my frame of reference had been too rigid. It could not stretch to absorb, much less explain or justify, the violation of my personal integrity by the surgical intervention. Under the impact of that outrage, my whole pattern of expectations broke like a brittle bone instead of expanding or bending to admit the new element. At college, my frame of reference was too flexible. I was indiscriminately receptive as if the body of my thought were boneless.

The backbone of a frame of reference, upon which everything else depends, consists of its doctrine of authority, its definition of what has the power and the right to command one's loyalty or assent. The authority in science is the consensus of qualified scientists, the qualifications being determined by the community of practising scientists. The authority in the American home is likely to be anyone who seizes it. The authority in much contemporary philosophy is the detached rational intellect. In traditional theology, the ostensible authority is usually God, but since theologians rarely agree in any detail on what God says or on how his self-disclosures are made and to be interpreted, the effectual authorities nearly always turn out to be something else: the Bible or tradition or personal experience or systematic consistency or one of the other disciplines such as science or history. It is comparatively easy to find and follow authorities in limited fields: the specialist in diseases of the heart, the recognized expert on information retrieval by computers, the master of symbolism. It can be supremely difficult to find an over-all authority that will bring these secondary authorities together into one comprehensive scheme that is both stable and pliant, firmly rooted in the ground and receptive to fresh experience.

For the moment, my authority was frankly my own sense of the fitness of things. I accepted Dr. MacLeod's authority on the importance and validity of my question because what he had to say about it rang true to me. I rejected other authorities whose credentials were equally impressive because what they said did not ring true to me. The standard was not only personal but private, and it cannot be justified except as a starting point — although for that purpose there is much to say in its favor. In practice, this is where all except slavish thought does begin: with the shock of recognizing that an idea or event or person rings true. Philosophers call such ideas "self-evident", and punctiliously remind us that since what is self-evident to one person may not be at all self-evident to anyone else, we are on slippery ground when we argue for the universal acceptance of a standard or proposition on the basis that it is self-evidently true.

But the objections to the use of self-evidence as a standard did not deter me, because I found all other standards equally objectionable for various other reasons, and this one at least held a measure of personal satisfaction.

4. *A Question of Integrity*

In marshalling my forces to find or create a frame of reference massive enough to provide me with support, and flexible enough to allow me to grow, my main guide was a passion for order. I wanted — I obstinately insisted on having — a *universe*, a coherent whole whose separate parts were integrated without violating the peculiar identity of each particular part, and in which every individual thing had meaning because of its relationship with a meaningful whole. Only an order of this kind, I felt, could bring emotion and reason into a union that protected the essential virtues of each. Dissociated, as I found them to be in psychology and philosophy as well as in myself, they were like a bachelor and spinster occupying the same house: sometimes comfortable together, sometimes in conflict, but never fruitfully joined.

Before my first conversation with Dr. MacLeod, I had almost abandoned my vision of an ultimate coherence because I found it impossible to accept the forms of it which I happened to be acquainted with. In grossly over-simplified terms, these consisted of a rationalism that appeared to renounce the personal life, and a personalism that appeared to reject rationality. To accept either threatened death by amputation, and the only combinations of them that I knew threatened death by civil war.

My commitment to a universal coherence was not — and is not — grounded in the authority of the Bible, or of any church, or of the Christian faith, or of a philosophical system. It was — and is — the manifestation of a fundamental choice, not an inference from some more basic conviction. Moreover, it was — and is — independent of others' convictions. So far as I was concerned, if any of the standard authorities happened to agree with my intuitive predilection, so much the better for them — they now had an ally — but I cared nothing for their claims. Certainly I was willing to grant that they might suggest fruitful lines of inquiry, and my willingness to learn from Christianity is attested by the heavily annotated margins and end papers in my copy of Dr. Henry B.

Sharman's *The Records of the Life of Jesus* which was our textbook for the discussion group led by Dr. MacLeod.

And I drew deeply on other sources to sustain my choice. The Quaker unprogrammed meeting for worship and the concerts of the Philadelphia Symphony Orchestra steadily nourished me. Poetry was a major support: "Life never was bonded to be endurable or the act of dying unpainful" . . . "The world stands out on either side / No wider than the heart is wide" . . . "Day unto day uttereth speech. What if the whole night spoke?" In philosophy, especially under Dr. Brand Blanshard, I beheld standards of rational coherence and of that excellent simplicity and proportion which is called "elegance", against which I still measure my own thought to my perennial shame. From other persons, both faculty and students, I gained wealth less easy to inventory but no less important. What none of them gave me, however, was the one thing I needed: a pattern or principle or structure that was not only coherently and elegantly ordered, but also inclusive, something capable of integrating all existence and experience, making possible the coherent interaction of passion and reason, and resulting in graciousness of living as well as a graceful economy of thought.

The belief that the entire universe is ordered coherently and elegantly cannot be proved by observation, experiment, logical procedures, or any other techniques known to man. Neither can it be disproved. No matter which side one takes, arguments and evidence can readily be found to support his case, and proponents of the opposite view will submit arguments and evidence that cannot be refuted. Rationally — and by "rational" I mean the intellect disengaged from any personal, moral, aesthetic, or religious considerations — there is no ground for cleaving to one rather than the other, so that the choice between them must be made on a non-rational basis. However, since both positions are defensible by reason — the intellect taking account of personal, moral, aesthetic, and religious considerations as well as rational ones — the choice of either is reasonable.

The catch in the business is that we must take one position or the other. We must presuppose ultimate coherence or ultimate incoherence. Like the actor confronting Ionesco's stage direction, "He either kisses or does not kiss Mrs. Smith," we can do either, but not both and not neither. We may not be aware of the problem, or we may not analyze it in this way, or we may change our position from one moment to the next. Still, when the instant for action comes — when the actor is on the stage — the commitment is made. The actor does or does not kiss Mrs. Smith, and we behave as if the universe were or were not coherently ordered.

As long as the problem is held in the realm of conjecture, we can be agnostics about it. Nothing in the sheer logic of the situation compels us to commit ourselves even temporarily, so that if we could live in a world of pure thought, we could indefinitely postpone the decision. But living requires us to act, and an act cannot be neutral. As I noted in the back of one of my books, "The necessity for action and decision has as a direct and necessary outcome integration of the individual. You must be integrated — at least for the moment — in order to decide."

Such decisions are not always consciously or directly made. Only when I look back upon myself-at-eighteen can I define in so many words the standards of inclusiveness, coherence, and elegance that I then adopted, or trace how the Gestalt psychology I was then studying influenced my thinking in another way: by creating a cast of mind. It is significant that I did not decide to major in psychology because I wanted to become a professional psychologist. I elected that major because in the Gestalt approach, and there only, I found attitudes, methods, and presuppositions which seemed to hold some promise of an intellectual integration that might finally develop into personal integrity.

Consequently, it was through my undergraduate work in psychology that I learned the disciplines of thinking in terms of dynamic interactions rather than of fixed essences, and in terms of functions, relationships, and contexts rather than of immutable and exactly determinable states. I grew accustomed to the fact that as we cannot see anything except from some particular physical position, we cannot think about anything except from a particular intellectual position, and that physically and intellectually we are constantly in flux. Thus we cannot state unequivocally either that the earth moves about the sun or the sun about the earth. All we can do is to choose a point of reference or a system of co-ordinates, then describe the motions by referring to that more or less arbitrarily chosen standard. And we can adopt different standards at different times or for different purposes. Presumably there is one astronomical event, the change in the relative positions of the sun and the earth, but since it cannot be perceived or analyzed except from a specific point of vantage, it cannot be known or interpreted neutrally or objectively or absolutely.

Over and over, in seminars on perception and learning, it was demonstrated that we are not passive recipients of sense impressions, and that the world does not interpret itself for our benefit. The nearest we can come to the ideal of detached scientific objectivity is when we recognize who we are and where we stand, and similarly make allowance for such factors when we are evaluating the observations of others. Even so, the pooling of our observations and resources cannot release us entirely from our limitations, because of the likelihood that we shall disregard not only the exceptionally obtuse but also the exceptionally penetrating vision. Neither individually nor socially can we escape ourselves. We are always involved in what we know. Therefore we must take ourselves into account when we construct our world views, both as a limiting factor (we cannot get outside ourselves) and as an enlarging one (we include ourselves in the picture).

Also through my teachers of Gestalt psychology, I began to see the distinction between a balance of powers, such as emotion and intellect, and an integration of powers. Balance implies an alternation, a collaboration of diverse elements, perhaps a compromise. Integrity, however, implies a union. The wayward heart and the disciplined mind no longer strain for equilibrium or subside into neutrality, but purged of their wilfulness, they become one. In that state, emotion and reason do not merely cooperate; they are conjoined as perception and memory are conjoined in the single flash of recognition. Their union is accomplished not by adding one to the other, but by cross-fertilizing each other so that the product is not an aggregate but a new creation.

Poets and novelists, it seems, know this quality of life better than psychologists and philosophers — at least they communicate it more often and more vividly. All careful observers, however, agree that most of us are not capable of sustaining the union of passion and lucidity as a habit of life, although many of us may attain it briefly, and that we abort the process of integration if we try to enforce the unity upon ourselves prematurely. Still, it is well to see that there is a difference between balance and integration, lest we set our sights too low.

The irrational but reasonable impulse toward inclusiveness, involvement, and integrity finally led me out of the fields of psychology, philosophy, and zoology, and into theology because theology explicitly includes everything within its purview, and insists that the person is an integral part of the whole he is studying. Many of the questions which theologians ask, of course, can be discussed in exclusively rational terms or become the subjects for anti-rational outbursts: good examples are the purely logical analysis of religious language, and the antipathy in some circles to the objective examination of religious faith or doctrines at all. But while theology has its full share of logic-choppers, the great theological arguments take place between persons who are in imminent peril of death, or who have never forgotten how close they once came to it.

Paul, Augustine, Luther, Calvin, Kierkegaard — in each of them, the vital need can be discerned behind their most speculative writings. Their lives and the lives of others are at stake, so they cannot afford to be merely abstract or visionary or one-track-minded. Their theologies must be inclusive, embracing as much of life and knowledge as the implacable mind together with the compassionate heart can grasp. They must also be coherent, with evidence and reasoning connected meaningfully to one another and to the whole pattern of their thought: beauty with truth, logic with ecstasy, the conclusions drawn from detached observation with the intuitions of the mystic, the world view of joy with the world view of despair. They are concerned with life in its entirety: mathematical physics and fairy tales, falling in love and the recondite meditations of philosophers, the practices of art and of common sense, individual and social structures, the facts of earthquakes, economics, and adoration. And in so far as a problem is treated theologically, it draws into itself evidence from all sources: observation, experiment, imagination, intuition, abstraction, reflection, aesthetic perception, and every other form of experience.

Although everything is relevant to theology, some things are more important than others, and one of the most serious problems for any theologian is to determine degrees of importance so as to obtain a just proportion within his theology. Theologians differ in such judgments, and the early and late work of a single theologian may vary widely in the emphasis given to a specific experience, problem, or premise. These alterations may reflect a deplorable inconsistency, or a solid development from a narrow or superficial world view to increasing breadth and profundity. In my own case, the experience and problem that constituted my jumping-off place remained central for a relatively short time. My initial premises proved to be more durable.

5. *A Basis for Operation*

In deciding that for the time being I would not commit suicide, I committed myself to answering a question, not to affirming a proposition or dogma. While obviously I could not foresee the consequences of my commitment, I knew that I was acting on the basis not of demonstration but of decision, and I was responsible for that decision. In other matters I might be the plaything of Fate or the hapless pawn of my heredity and environment, but here I was not.

I knew also that in my search for an answer, I was starting with certain assumptions about the nature of the world and of knowledge. A few months after my initial conference with Dr. MacLeod, I undertook the salutary exercise of writing down what those assumptions were. I entitled the product, "Creed," and filed it in the notebook where I kept my poetry.

> I believe in myself — within limitations.
> I believe in others — some of them.
> I believe only this: that there is an ultimate truth, a reason for life, and that by living as strongly and as beautifully as it is in me to live, and by searching for it, I will someday know what that truth is.
> This is the only thing in which I implicitly believe.
> It is not enough, but it will grow.

Naïve though it was, and clumsy and only half-expressed, the formula contained three salient points whose importance I perceived immediately, and a fourth whose significance I did not grasp until much later. I was assuming first that the universe is ordered; second, that by the interplay of action and reflection I could discover the nature of that order; and third, that the order could be recognized by its inclusiveness, coherence, and elegance.

None of these assumptions can be proved to be true. Any order that the universe appears to have may well be the product of the ordering mind, a pattern imposed by the intellect upon the evidence rather than discerned within it. To go farther back, the universe may not exist at all apart from our ideas about it. As every student of philosophy learns in his elementary course, there is no rational justification for the leap from idea to existence, from "I think" to "I am". Therefore I was beginning my journey with standards that were, to say the least, questionable, and I was perfectly well aware of it. One must, however, start somewhere. One cannot think at all without assuming something: a reasonably faithful correspondence between ideas and things, or no such correspondence; the existence of a real world and one's own reality, or no such realities. So consciously and deliberately, I leaped.

When as a college sophomore I wrote my literally sophomoric creed, the fourth of its implicit assumptions completely escaped my attention: the prevailing attitude of skepticism. In its first two sentences, I voiced the belief that I could not depend entirely on myself — my motives, intentions, abilities, perceptions, reasoning, or anything else — or upon others. My skepticism was originally a defiance that had its source in despair. It became much later a settled conviction and fountainhead of hope. Meanwhile, it saved me from what I now consider to be the deadliest peril that man — any man — faces: the dogmatic confidence in human ability to live with complete adequacy, whether in the world of nature, in society, or in his central self. With Gottfried, in Romain Rolland's *Jean-Christophe,* I believed that those who boast, " 'He who wills, can' . . . are liars, or else they do not will anything much."

Probably my distrust of human perfection and perfectability was a projection of my unconscious feelings of inadequacy, and by turning my sense of inferiority into a universal principle, I was trying to moderate its painful impact: misery loves company. I do not question the accuracy of that explanation so far as it refers to the genesis of my skepticism. The validity of an idea, however, is not determined by its source. An imbecile can speak the truth; the wisest of men can err. A rationally impeccable argument can lead to a wrong conclusion if it is developed from false premises; a sound conclusion can be reached by an improper chain of reasoning. It may help in understanding a theology to know that it was fashioned under one or another condition of personal stress, but it is no more significant in appraising the system than the value of Poincaré's mathematical contributions is determined by learning that one of his most important insights came to him at the moment when he was stepping onto a streetcar. The circumstances surrounding the act of discovery, and the truth of the discovery, are separate items, and to confuse them is to commit the error known to logicians as the genetic fallacy.

In this connection, it is worth noting that those who do place their ultimate faith in man have almost certainly reached their position by the same method I used in reaching my contrary faith. So if the psychological interpretation is followed, we cancel each other out. Their belief has its source in experiences where they found themselves and others dealing adequately with the situations they met, and from such experiences they have derived the happy assurance of human sufficiency, or the less happy but equally strong assurance that they can legitimately disallow those problems that are not susceptible to human efforts. While often much of their hope lies in the expectation that men of the future can accomplish what they and their contemporaries cannot, they are still affirming either that any question a man can ask, a man will sooner or later be able to answer, or that the problem has been wrongly conceived. Their experience, however, no more proves the validity of their position than my experience proves the validity of mine. The source of an idea can suggest its personal significance and transmit its personal meaning, but does not guarantee its truth.

Between these positions, ultimate trust in and distrust of man, a great gulf is fixed, nowhere more evident than in my judgment that the humanist is unconscionably arrogant, and his that I am a craven defeatist. And each of us, of course, believes the other to be the victim of despair. He says, "We have this hope or none at all." I reply, "If this be our hope, then we are lost indeed."

During my years at Swarthmore, such hope as I had was concentrated on an indefinite power or activity or process that I called "Life", and conceived of as setting before us an infinite number of possibilities of which some are forced upon us and others are permanently closed to us. Of the almost infinite remainder, we have not time enough for exploring or using all that we are capable of grasping. We must select, even though each "yes" to one thing requires a "no" to something else. To accept the joys of marriage is to refuse the joys of celibacy. To affirm that all life is coherent is to deny that any part of it is ultimately incoherent. Because we know only as we can, we are imprisoned by our finitude. Yet our prison is larger than the cells where we are individually confined, and the walls that divide us can become supports for stairways that will surmount them. While we are all invincibly ignorant, we are not ignorant about the same things, so that when we scale the walls between our private cells we become less circumscribed than we were, even if the process does not release us from all restraint.

For this reason, the fundamental proposition, "We know only as we can," does not justify complacency or inaction. What it does is to encourage a decent humility. To be humble, however, does not mean to be passive or anxious or, in Charles Williams' phrase, "to think yourself a worm". The word humble comes from the Latin *humus:* earth, soil, ground. Our physical lives are tied to the soil through the food we must have to sustain our bodies, and all our experience indicates that bodies are necessary for the functioning of reason, emotion, and will. Therefore our most subtle dialectics, our most elevated visions, our most penetrating analyses, are nourished by the dust under our feet.

In areas of study like mathematics and some branches of philosophy, it is permissible to leave this characteristic out of account, but no one — however erudite — can leave it out of his life, and no theologian can leave it out of his daily work. No matter how remote his discussion may sound, always he is tied to the complex and changing mixture, the humus, within and from which his thinking grows and to which it finally refers: not only the physiological conditions for living, but also the personal relationships, the social milieu, the resources of art and tradition, and all the other practical and theoretical elements that together form the ground for human living. He is not dealing only with polished and sterilized nuggets — numbers or pure cases or words having one exact definition and no connotations at all. At the beginning and end of the day, his hands are in the fertile soil.

I began my theological journey and established my basis of operation long before I knew what theology is or that I was theologizing. Yet by the end of my senior year in college, my theological standards and techniques were fairly well established: what rings true to me; coherence, inclusiveness, and elegance; the provisional hope, acquired from Dr. MacLeod, that the life of Jesus was as good a place as any to find the key to living, and better than some. I remember his saying that while one could start with peanuts to learn the meaning of life and the way to live, it would take longer than starting with Jesus because in studying peanuts, the decisive questions for human life were not posed so directly.

So far I had little more than a basis of operation, and it was not a bad basis even though I could not have formulated it then as clearly as I can now. Then I could see only a few flecks of light in an aboriginal darkness, and I had no way of knowing which were fugitive and which were stable, or where any of them might lead.

chapter three

THE SPLITTING OF HAIRS

The world's in the devil's own mess chiefly because it has forgotten that some hairs have to be split.
CHARLES MORGAN, *The Judge's Story*

1. *A Conflict of Authorities*

"Here, in me, there is nothing but desolation and barrenness." So I wrote in my journal a year after my graduation from college. I had intended to go on to graduate school for research in the psychology of religion, and had applied for fellowships to the two universities that offered what I wanted. Both schools named me as the alternate. Not having enough money of my own to support myself without a scholarship, I went home into a hell of recrimination, guilt, and frustration.

My parents had paid for my college education on the explicit understanding that I should equip myself to be self-supporting and that immediately upon graduation I should begin to earn my own living. I had chosen my curriculum, however, in terms of my intrinsic interests instead of the vocational utility of the courses, with the innocent trust that I would be able to find a job when the time came for it. Thus I graduated from college prepared for nothing except graduate school, and with no desire for anything except further academic work — and that not at once. For a variety of reasons (including my decision to break an engagement to be married), I was lacerated in mind and spirit, and needed time to heal.

Because my father had died suddenly in 1937, the issue was fought out between my mother and myself, and "fought" is the correct word. She saw me turning into a feckless nonentity determined to sponge upon her as long as she was irresponsible enough to allow me to do so. Hitherto I had shown few signs of stability and dependability, and she felt that she would be failing in her bounden duty if she encouraged my perverse determination to drift along in my own way. Therefore she used every weapon at her command — and she had many — in attacking my resolution to collect myself for a year and then to prepare for teaching and research.

Against her I was all but defenseless because I readily admitted the force of her accusations. I knew I was guilty of breaking my contract to be self-supporting. I could see for myself the dangers I was skirting by delay in settling down to a job: I had been frightened by them before she spelled out the details for my benefit. I was desperately conscious of my ignorance of the world, and desperately apprehensive about my ability to cope with it. Therefore I could reply only with the plea for time, and for faith that in the long run I would prove myself to her satisfaction. But time was the one thing that in good conscience she could not permit me, and daily I was giving her additional reasons for distrusting my reliability.

Sometime during that winter or early spring, I gave in to the extent of hunting a job, but I could find none even remotely connected with my interests and training. When I extended my investigations to cover any work whatsoever, still I failed. These were the years of the Great Depression, and like many of my betters I could find no job at all, although soon I would have done anything which would liberate me from the house for a few hours of the day. What finally turned up was a post as apprentice medical technologist in the laboratory of a hospital a few blocks from my home. It paid nothing, but it held the promise of ultimate financial independence, and it more or less satisfied Mother. Also, it all but destroyed me as a person.

The work and the people I worked with were interesting and sometimes enjoyable, and my superiors praised my work. But I could not rid myself of the feeling that when I accepted the job, I had violated my personal integrity and betrayed the vocation, as yet not defined, for which I had been made. Consequently, when a series of fortuitous events resulted in the offer of a scholarship to Chicago Theological Seminary, I broke my promise to stay at the hospital for at least a year, and set forth to find out what "religionists" (as I then rather condescendingly called them) thought religion was, in preparation for the study of its psychology.

To Mother, the breaking of this second contract was final proof of my irresponsibility, and she protested bitterly against my decision. For three days, neither she nor my sister and brother would so much as ask me to pass the salt. I defended the decision on the ground that since I would no longer be financially dependent upon her (the scholarship was adequate to cover all my expenses in Chicago for that year), I was fulfilling the spirit of the original contract to support myself. Upon that grievously unsatisfactory basis, I left home and never again returned there to live.

Mother and I were splitting hairs, of course. But let those who decry the splitting of hairs take note of what was involved. Our honesty and good faith. Our accuracy and clarity of reasoning. Our definitions of rights and responsibilities within the family, and thereby the nature of society and of man. Looking back, I cannot blame or commend either of us. Each acted according to the light she had, only my light was her darkness, and her light was darkness for me.

At least we did not separate over a trivial issue. The keeping or breaking of a contract can be well worth fighting about. Some hairs need to be split, as ought to be obvious from the most cursory observation of our ordinary work and recreation. An inaccuracy of one ten thousandth of an inch in one part of an airplane can send a hundred people plummeting to their deaths. Infinitesimal variations of muscular control determine our pleasure or disappointment in a concert or athletic performance. The impact of a letter may depend upon the elusive connotations of a single word. As the balance of foods can make the difference between health and malnutrition, so the balance of facts, their weighting and arrangement, can lead to truth or error. Considering the extent to which hair-splitting affects our daily lives in decisive and conspicuous ways, it is both amusing and appalling how frequently theology is damned for being "nothing but the splitting of hairs", as if that activity were neither interesting nor important.

The theological meaning of the split in this particular hair will not be rightly understood unless it is recognized that my mother's stand was entirely reasonable, and that I knew it to be more reasonable than my own. We had discussed the reasons at agonizing length and had consulted outside authorities: trusted friends of the family, a doctor, a psychiatrist, anyone whose position or experience led either of us to hope for soundly objective advice. Nearly all of them agreed that my decision to leave home was a sign of inexcusable naïveté, impulsiveness, and ingratitude. They stated that conclusion intelligently, basing it on so wide a knowledge of the world, and usually with so loving a concern, that I felt unprincipled and impious in resisting them.

Having no answers to their objections, no arguments to adduce for my own case (a steadfast intuition does not constitute an argument), and no guide but my unsubstantiated conviction of what was right for me, I was wretchedly uncertain of what I ought to do, and wretchedly certain that I would suffer terribly if I made a mistake here, even though the error were made in good faith. On the one side stood myself, my touchstone being the incommunicable and indefensible criterion of what rang true to me. On the other side stood Mother, with reason, worldly knowledge, and a host of advisers around her. Whose truth was true — hers or mine? To find an authority surmounting our conflicting authorities became an imperative practical need. But how could we find such an authority? What single truth could reconcile our separate truths? What is truth?

I did not know what the truth was. I was sure that neither of us had the whole truth, but which of us had the more was beyond my capacity to determine. So far as I could discover, it was beyond anyone's capacity. None the less, I had to follow Mother's definition or my own. I could either bestow upon her the authority to direct my life, yielding the responsibility for it to her; or I could assert my own authority and take on a responsibility that I was not at all confident of being able to carry without her moral and financial support. In one way there was no choice. I could not have permitted her to define my truth without ceasing to be a responsible person, or indeed a person at all. In another way, this was the choice of all choices, the ultimate point of freedom: to become a person or to become a satellite permanently tethered to standards of truth which I would have to follow blindly and dumbly because they were not my own. To complicate matters still further, I could not express my responsibility to myself without denying my responsibility to my employers and my family.

I was on the train and well on my way to Chicago before I

realized unconditionally, in a flood of joy that surged up through a flood of tears, that while I was partly in the wrong by leaving home, I was essentially and astonishingly right.

We do not know what "The Truth" is. We decide what we will live by, what will be true for us. Some years later when the existentialist affirmation, "That is truth which is true for me," came to my attention, I had no hesitation about accepting it. My struggle over leaving home, however, prevented me from ever supposing that "truth for me" could possibly be identified with "absolutely and universally True." My truth was only my truth, not Mother's or anyone else's. Conceivably she and I might sometime reach agreement on that issue (to anticipate: we did. Ultimately, I think, she agreed that I had been right), in which case we could say, "This is our truth," an improvement over the individual "my truth", but still not "The Truth" — final, absolute, and one.

2. *An Ambiguous Authority*

During the months when I was involved in the conflict of authorities, another strand of experience was confirming even more explicitly the judgment that in the end, one does not discover what "The Truth" is, but decides what shall be true for him.

A good many times, that year, I escaped at night from the house by crawling out of my bedroom window onto the slanting porch roof outside it, there to see in the stars and feel on the wind the freedom I could not possess. During those sessions, I sometimes found myself praying to a God — not because I believed in any such being, but because I was at the end of my rope and I had to do something. There was nothing within or around me on which I could depend for help, but if the universe contained no source of help at all, it was a chaos and I was condemned to the chaos of insanity. My choice lay between a God who was independent of me and of the world's judgments, and chaos, and I fought chaos as instinctively and violently as I have fought every general anaesthetic I have ever been given.

Irrationally and unreasonably, as first expectation and then hope died under attack, I clutched at the supposition that while all things in the universe might conspire separately against me, the universe as a whole was not antagonistic. The frame of reference which is greater than the sum of its parts, or the pivot on which that framework swung, was not hostile. It held its majestic course, destroying whatever contravened "the army of unutterable law" and supporting whatever cooperated with it. Things appeared to be my enemies only because I had not found my proper place among them.

It may be possible to pray to a universal frame of reference or a pivot or a moral imperative. Without doubt it is possible to pray to a hypothetical God. In my extremity, however, all questions of possibility and definition went by the board. I prayed because I was drained and sucked dry, without efficacy or vitality or resource within myself. I prayed to a God because I had no friend or associate who would listen to me and take me seriously as a person. I imagined God as beyond the world because the world which I knew did not contain any resources to help me. I was confronting God or nothingness, and having no conclusive proof that a God did not exist, I assumed a God in order to have something to pray to. "Give me this day my daily bread," I implored night after night. "Give me something to live on, something to hang onto. Show me what to do."

The first effect of that prayer was to turn my gaze outward. Assuming a God outside myself, I assumed that any answer would appear outside me. My study of the Gospels under Dr. MacLeod and his teacher, Dr. Sharman, had left me with the suspicion that like Jesus' disciples, I might not recognize truth when it was set before me, so it was imperative that I keep constant watch for its arrival and be alert for whatever form it might take.

It is impossible to demonstrate that the sustenance I received was given me by any God in response to any prayer, but I did receive sustenance. An unexpected smile by a patient from whom I was taking a blood sample carried me through one especially bitter day; the design made by a branch of a tree against the sky carried me through another. I had prayed for nourishment; I was nourished. Did the food come from God, or from nature, or from my having turned to look outward upon the world rather than inward upon myself? Here was another hair that had to be split. Granting that I was nourished, what was the source of that daily bread?

The fact that one event — I prayed for help — was followed by another event — I was helped — does not prove that the first caused the second. They may have been related only by concomitant variation, as a person may consistently read a newspaper while he eats breakfast, but the reading does not cause him to eat or the eating cause him to read. The events regularly coincide but have no necessary connection with each other. When two events invariably appear together, we are apt to conclude that there is a chain of cause and effect between them, but even so, it is often difficult to determine which is cause and which is effect. Is chronic physical fatigue, for instance, the cause or effect of emotional disturbance? How can we determine which diagnosis is correct? If we treat only the body or only the mind, and both respond favorably, the cure may indicate nothing more than that in breaking a vicious cycle, it does not always matter where the break is made.

In the case of prayer, the problem is more difficult because without exception (so far as I know), all "answers" to prayer can be adequately explained by reference to something other than a "divine reply". Spontaneous cures of inoperable cancer occur only rarely, but the irreligious seem to benefit from them as often as the religious. Talking problems over with a sympathetic person frequently seems to be as effective in relieving immoderate tension as praying to a god. The psychological phenomenon of insight, in perception and learning, has many features in common with what are called "religious revelations", and atheists and theists may not differ except in detail on the conclusions they reach by what they call respectively "insight" and "revelation".

Theologians and scientists alike are apt to use Occam's razor for splitting this particular hair: if there are several sufficient explanations for an event, one should take the simplest. Unfortunately, that principle does not automatically determine whether it is simpler to postulate a natural or a supernatural cause for the effects of prayer, or whether — since the effects may be much the same either way — it makes any real difference which explanation we choose. When healing, the relief of alienation, and the improvement of human conditions are available without prayer, why bother with it except as a form of entertainment? This question needs to be answered in terms of a deeper one: what is the function of prayer?

At that time and in those circumstances, I understood prayer to be a method of causing things to happen. Intellectually, I was working with a mechanical model derived from the naïve supposition that all mental and physical events can be attributed to precise causal antecedents, and that every cause has precisely predictable effects. Since A and B together produce C, if C occurs then A and B must have been present to beget it. If fervent prayer were in any sense an effective force, it would generate an answer. If I received an answer, it would be because I had prayed. If I did not receive an answer, it would be either because I had not prayed long or sincerely enough, or because I had failed to identify the answer when it was given.

My practice was better than my theory. At rock bottom, I did not expect that my prayers would change anything or cause anything to happen. I am not even sure that I wanted any such effects. What I did want, and hardly dared hope for, was a response: some evidence that the universe or something in the universe would respond to a human cry. I wanted to know that my call was answered not by the echo of my own voice but by another voice. Its utterance might not convey any more information than Yahweh's discourse to Job, but it would testify that I was heard. So while nothing would be added to my experience, everything would be transformed.

The function of prayer which my practice implied, therefore, was not that of mechanical causation but of personal responsiveness. Indeed I wanted my situation to be altered and I wanted to be told what to do. But even more desperately, I wanted to know that I was not alone. The appropriate analogy, on the purely human level, is with asking a question of another human being. The inquiry may elicit a reply; it does not cause the reply. The categories of cause and effect are irrelevant here.

I believed and still believe that the nourishment that came to me was not an effect of my prayer for daily bread, but a response to it. My entreaty provided the occasion for a reply; it did not compel the outcome in the way that a cause compels an effect. I am convinced that the response came from outside myself because it was so completely unexpected, both in the manner of its appearance and in its adequacy. I did not receive any sign; my problems were not solved; my mother did not alter her position; I was not provided with a chart of my future. Instead I was encouraged — infused with courage — to choose which way I should take rather than to succumb to the pressures focussed upon me. I was not guided, I was freed. Yet even that response was not straightforward or unmistakable, but permeated throughout with ambiguity. Its response might mean almost anything. Its source might be natural or supernatural.

For the moment, as a working hypothesis, I took the response as coming from a supernatural source because that was what it appeared to be, and therefore seemed simpler than predicating a natural phenomenon under a supernatural guise. Thanks to Occam's razor, I found myself accepting as my Lord an ambiguous authority of which I knew only that it — or he — did respond, however ambiguously, when I called upon him.

3. *The Individual and the Personal*

In seminary, at first I shied away from courses in theology because my philosophy seminars in college had sickened me of what I then felt to be rationalistic quibbling about inconsequential issues, and I expected that theology would consist of more and worse of the same. Two persons gentled my apprehensions: my professor of church history, Dr. Matthew Spinka, who made the ancient theological controversies live for me by demonstrating how they grew out of such difficulties as those I was facing, and a senior student, Emerson W. Shideler, who assured me that theology dealt directly with the great problems of living. By Christmas, I had begun to suspect that I might not be in seminary the following year but instead would be married, so I took the calculated risk of failing a course that first year students were strongly advised not to take, and registerd for Dr. E. E. Aubrey's "Outlines of Christian Theology."

Dr. Aubrey taught his course by lecturing on five topics: knowledge, God, man, society, and salvation. Under each heading he presented the various traditional positions without declaring his own. The students were required to supplement the lectures with extensive reading, and at the end of the quarter to write a paper stating and defending their own theologies. My paper — a theological dialogue — ended: "The answers [I have found] are probably wrong; they usually are, but thank God I'm aware of the problems."

Although I attempted in the paper to maintain a fair degree of detachment and objectivity, I stated explicitly at the beginning that what I was trying to work out was not a universal theology, but a particular one based on my individual experiences. I felt that until I had ordered my own intellectual and spiritual household, I was in no position to cope with anything broader. Consequently, the essay was shamelessly egocentric. The problems were *my* problems. The authority I sought was to be an authority for *me*. The attitudes I was expressing were *mine*. Every section started or ended with what *I* could or could not believe, egocentrically exhibiting my awareness of being an individual who was equipped with a singular set of capacities and who had been produced by reacting to a singular combination of pressures. These capacities and pressures were shared by others, but their proportion in me was unique. Therefore I was an island unto myself, like every other individual. None of my experiences could be wholly shared; all my problems and solutions were partly secret; my theology, like all others, was irremediably private, relevant only to its creator.

Had this position been a theoretical one, I might well have stopped there. So far as I can discover, there is no way out of the egocentric predicament by rational thought or by observation. All the major streams of traditional Western thought — rationalism, empiricism, mysticism, skepticism, positivism — are blocked at this point. But I was not coolly comparing systems. I was fighting for my life. I had to have help from outside myself, but being a unique individual, I was cut off from the other unique individuals who might have helped me, as they were cut off from any help I might have given them. We were indeed joined by our common humanity, but humanity in itself does not generate union among human beings. As often as not, it produces mutual destructiveness. It seemed that if in the end my individuality were to be preserved, I should have to abandon any profound intercommunion with my fellows, but if I surrendered to my insatiable hunger for community, I should have to sacrifice my identity as an individual.

As so often happens in theology, the practical solution to the dilemma preceded any theoretical formulation. Through my seminary studies, I discovered that for all the individual disparities separating me from Irenaeus and Tertullian and Augustine of Hippo and others of the early Fathers, we did in fact meet with an unmistakable intimacy. As individuals, Augustine (for example) and I are so unlike that we could almost be said to belong to different species. It is fantastic — the stuff of fantasy — to think that he could speak to me or I reply to him across the abysses of time, space, culture, historical setting, temperament, sex, education, and ability that divide us. For that matter, considering the extent to which his theology grew directly out of incidents and ingredients peculiar to himself, it is astonishing that he could speak to anyone else at all. In fact, however, he does. His passion awakes that of many others, and our passion finds a response in him.

According to the philosophies and psychologies I knew, such immediate confrontation is impossible. Our "meeting" must have been an illusion evoked by my imagination working on my need. Essentially I must have been creating an imaginary playmate from the material of Augustine's autobiography and theology. What I heard in his voice was the reflection of my own. By attributing my sensations and ideas to him, or his to myself, I must have been hiding from myself the caustic reality of my isolation in the egocentric predicament.

There was, however, another remote possibility, although at the time I had no idea of what it might imply or where it might lead: that the egocentric predicament constituted only one part of the total situation. Occam's convenient razor might be employed to prompt the suggestion that what seemed true — my finding in Augustine an ally and companion — was actually true, and the complicated hypothesis of the psychologists, that by devious operations of the unconscious I was projecting myself upon him, was false.

I find no more justification for doubting the reality of my encounter with Augustine and other ancient worthies than for doubting my similar meetings with a number of other persons whom I have known solely through the written word: for instance, correspondents with whom I have exchanged letters for years but whom I have never met face to face. It is true that written words can be misunderstood, but so can spoken words, gestures, and facial expressions. My epistolary friends can answer my direct questions, but so can Augustine if I am as careful with him as with my contemporaries in making inquiries appropriate to their concerns and within the scope of their competence. He has no word for me on nuclear warfare; neither, it happens, do most of my acquaintances on the relation between the ideal Church and actual churches. There is no substitute for intelligence in personal dealings of any kind. With them, as with him, the bond of union is our personal involvement with a common set of problems. Each of us as an individual is separately engaged in a search or battle or pursuit which is basically the same for us all, and into which we have thrown ourselves not merely as individuals, but as persons.

What is a "person", that Augustine and I could meet personally? I cannot define the word directly; all I can do is to talk around it, starting with a negative. Neither here nor elsewhere do I mean by "personal" that cozy familiarity which is neither modest nor dignified, and by its indecent lack of reserve breeds not only contempt but disgust. Such rank emotionalism sometimes passes for personal relationship, but is in fact an aberration of persons because by definition, to be personal means that all the functions of the person are actively involved in the relation: intelligence as well as emotion, volition as well as preference, intention as well as motive, separation as well as union, individuality as well as communion. Nor does personal exchange depend upon affection or even face to face acquaintance. It is a matter of participation by whole and authentic persons.

The positive approach to personhood begins with the recognition that rightly or wrongly, for good or ill, we do distinguish between persons and things. Partly this is a matter of choice: we decide to treat our pet dog as a person, our neighbor's pet dog as a thing. We respond to a compliment with polite, impersonal detachment or with warm, personal exultation. Partly it is a matter of something less generally recognized: that certain beings and situations call forth from us the special kind of response that we call "personal". The child, luminous with joy, runs into our arms and cries, "I love you. Do you love me?" Then if we remain impersonal, we commit a brutality and we know it unless as persons we are dead. The poem, the symphony, the speaker, the painting, the building, awake in us a personal movement of approval or dislike, or do not touch us personally: they leave us cold. Things are known to be things by their contrast with persons; persons are known to be persons by their contrast with things.

Moreover, a thing — even a human infant — becomes a person only by being treated as a person and responding in kind. The quality of "person" is a characteristic acquired only by direct contagion. It is also a variable characteristic. Some beings (compare humans with insects) seem to have more capacity for personal development than others, and some individuals within a species grow farther in that direction than others.

The Splitting of Hairs

The distinction between person and thing is forced upon those of us whose native tongue is English, because we are compelled by its pronouns to make it. In referring to God, for example, I must speak either of "him" or of "it", or employ the unsatisfactory equivocation, "him (or it)". The language has no neutral pronoun by which I could indicate a being who is neither personal nor impersonal, and no inclusive pronoun for referring to something (someone) both personal and impersonal. Still more awkwardly, a personal being must be either male or female. In speaking, writing, and even in thinking, I am constrained by my native language to make a philosophical and theological dichotomy between personal and impersonal, and if personal, between male and female. I cannot specify neither or both without circumlocutions.

I am not at all comfortable about calling God a person: it is too limited a term. But to refer to God as a thing would be worse, suggesting a machine or a beast or an abstraction. I do not like the alternatives which the English language allows me, nor its requirement that I choose between them. Being faced with these possibilities, however, and no others, I must make a decision, and my decision not only expresses a theological position, but actively determines the course of my theological development.

As individuals, Augustine and I are utterly separate from each other. But we are also persons, and because the source and nature of personal life depend upon a process of transmission, as persons we can be united with each other. It is of the essence of personal communication that in it there is identity in diversity, union in separation; therefore our manifold barriers of individuality are transformed into bridges between us. The egocentric dead end becomes a personal highway. Complicated though it sounds, the achievement is common and often easy. It is the analysis which is difficult, as is almost invariably true of our simple and direct experiences.

Angels danced for me on the razor's edge where the individual and the personal converged and divided. I was not alone. I had never been alone. While I was struggling with my question, the theologians of old — and of the present — had been struggling with it. When I was lonely, they had been lonely: the recognition of our isolated state as individuals is apparently a necessary, or all but necessary, part of the way toward becoming

57

persons. They had understood the structure of my problems and had propounded answers that were intensely meaningful to me. And they had gone far beyond me in working out implications and organizing their ideas. What did it matter that Augustine had died almost a millennium and a half before I was born? He was my teacher and I his newest pupil, and life offers no more intimate relationship when what is taught and learned is personal.

And there was even more at stake. All the years since I had lost the religion of my childhood, I had believed that my struggles had taken me farther and farther from Christianity. Now I discovered — and with what amazement! — that they had brought me straight to its center. My early training had misled me, because Christian faith is not founded upon arbitrary pronouncements; it grows out of despair and questioning, insight and joy, like my own. Christian history is the record of my companions' efforts to heal our brokenness and establish our peace. Christian theology is not the logical defense of rigid doctrines, but the continuing labor to comprehend the whole range of life, and to act with wisdom and holiness. My individual search for a personal meaning had inducted me into a community. My skepticism had educated me in faith.

Appropriately, my membership in that community was marked with a sign: the three words preceding the grade Dr. Aubrey gave me on the term paper I wrote for him: "Since they insist: A." Since the university required that students be graded on their work, he would comply, but he would also attest his conviction that the grade was the least important feature of the enterprise for me as well as for him. He accepted me as belonging to the company of those who theologize because they care about what is going on, and will continue to theologize when all the courses for credit are finished.

4. *Faith and Freedom*

These same short months of my seminary studies contained another and quite different strand of my theological development: I was undergoing the critical experience of finding out what "faith" means, in the extreme sense which the contemplative tradition calls "unitive belief".

Ordinarily, by faith we mean the act of trusting, whether it be reasonable or unreasonable to rely on the object of our faith.

It is something we do. This, however, was something done to me. I was not accepting some person or process as a support to hold me up; it — whatever "it" might be — was setting me upright, lifting me as I might lift a child and set him upon his feet. Or in another figure, I was not travelling my own gait or by my own power; I was vividly conscious of being carried. I did not know who or what was doing this, or why, or how long it would last. My faith had no object that I could identify. It was enough, for the moment, to have it happen and to be exalted by it and to know that this is the end for which man was made: to be borne by something (someone), and in time to know his bearer.

That kind of faith cannot endure for long because I am not capable of retaining possession of it. My habit of directing and depending upon myself intervenes; or my natural impulse to hold onto the experience leads me to clutch it so tightly that it dies within my hands. We who are imperfect cannot keep the perfect gift, and could not even if it were given us — as it seems not to be, in this life — for keeps. Neither can we obtain it by reaching or asking. It is not a reward for merit but, so far as we can tell, an arbitrary benefaction, the wind of God that blows according to laws we do not comprehend and in a manner we cannot control. I wrote in my journal, "Conflict and sorrow and the deep misery of loneliness will come again, but I'm not afraid of them any more. Come soon or late, the gods or the God have given me this, and I am very grateful."

The experience of unitive belief contradicts the experience of despair, the one showing the world as a glory, the other disclosing it as a horror. Are the beauty and the ugliness in the eye of the beholder, or in the world he beholds? Is the world itself neutral, neither lovely nor dreadful, or does the indifferent eye function like the camera film that records a richly colored world in shades of grey? I had seen the colors, brilliant and subtle and somber. I had heard from others that they too perceived the world chromatically. I could not postulate a basically monochromatic or neutral world, even though I could see a number of important services that might be rendered by temporarily adopting a black-and-white vision — the etcher's view, one might call it — excluding the moral and emotional and aesthetic colors of reality in order to emphasize its formal design.

But when it came to affirming the ultimacy of the joyous or

the despairing world view, I had no rational basis for deciding between them. Those two metaphysical principles of interpretation were so balanced in my experience that I could not deny the validity of either. To me, both must be valid propositions, or neither, and if neither I was left with the neutrality I had already refused. But for the time being, I let the controversy take care of itself. Life was terrible and wonderful at once, and might be anything else it wanted to be for all I cared, because Emerson and I were getting married.

A year before our wedding, all doors had seemed to be closed against me. Now all doors seemed to be open, and I was intoxicated with my freedom. The odd thing about it, however, was that this freedom was the direct consequence of my binding myself for life to another person whom I did not know very well. We had agreed that for us, marriage should be irrevocable. On the inside of our rings is engraved not a date, and not initials, but the phrase "An eternal covenant". Whatever happened, we had resolved to stick it out — together.

"Whatever happened." "A person I did not know very well." I could not know Emerson well, because a person in a new relationship is necessarily to some degree a new person. Until he became my husband, I could not know what kind of a husband he would make. Neither could I find out what kind of a wife I would be for him without actually becoming his wife. As friends and fiancés we were thoroughly satisfied with each other, but marriage is not the same as friendship or engagement. Married, we were bound to each other. Yet it was the bondage itself that generated my freedom.

The most remarkable feature of that freedom was its identity with my recent experience of faith. In both cases I found myself being carried: earlier by an infinite, immutable power whose nature I could not perceive, much less comprehend; now by a finite, steadfast relation whose nature I could in part perceive and comprehend. Consequently, while I might still lament, as I had in college, "I don't know which way is up," as least I had discovered which way was down. Having a firm ground under my feet, I was no longer thrashing around in search of a foothold for my personal existence, and could stand or walk or run or dance as I chose. I could rest on the human ground of our marriage, and the marriage rested upon the bedrock of my unknown sustainer. Establishing a personal center, I was free to move personally in the same way that I am free to move physically on the globe of the earth: across its surface toward all the points of the compass, delving toward its heart, or ascending into the empyrean heights. So long as I knew where my center was, I could not be wholly lost. The experience of unitive belief had convinced me that the world had an ultimate center; my marriage gave me a definite habitation in relation to that center. Home was wherever Emerson and I were together.

No theological concept is more beset by contradictions than the doctrine of freedom. Two of the contradictions were peculiarly relevant to my condition during the months immediately after our wedding. First, my freedom appeared to be the result of a particular kind of bondage; and second, each of my free acts had increased my freedom by limiting it. These two discoveries — perceived at the time but not formulated until many years afterward — gave me my earliest insight into the style of living which I call "the way of indirection", in which certain ends are achieved only by applying one's efforts to something else.

Because we do not live in a vacuum but in a world where a thousand pressures pull and push us at every step, we are free only so far as we can assign precedence among them and so keep them in their places. That is, we can — within limits — decide which pressures we shall resist or ignore, and which we shall submit to. No man can serve two masters without breaching his integrity, but unless he serves one, he disintegrates. It is significant that we not only feel, but become in fact most free not when we are at loose ends, but when we are moving without serious hindrance toward an end that we have freely chosen or accepted, when we have tied ourselves down over the long or short run and thereby have liberated ourselves from distracting claims upon our time and energies. By focussing upon the one thing, we cease to be vulnerable to a great many other things, and are able to order the pressures that we cannot escape. Our self-imposed bondage gives us a negative freedom from the imperious demands of other lords.

Forced servitude is slavery. All of us live under some necessities: physical, biological, psychological, intellectual, social. Therefore it would seem that we are all slaves, and that the sense of positive freedom we occasionally enjoy is a delusion. If in nothing else, we are slaves of the necessity to choose among our conflicting impulses and needs, to determine which we shall satisfy at any given moment. Yet in the midst of our most straitened captivity, we have one crucial point of utter freedom. We can choose between resenting or resisting our necessities, and using them in the service of the ends we have freely chosen to follow. We can hate our necessities or love them.

The hitch, of course, is that great necessities cannot serve trivial ends. Irremediable bodily pain cannot contribute much if anything to the goal of improving one's social status, except perhaps in a highly specialized community like a hospital ward. It is possible, however, to use physical agony as a means for approaching a transcendent end, such as unveiling the glories of human and divine compassion. No pain, no limitation, needs to be useless or meaningless, and if we use our necessities as gifts, we become their masters.

Even so, in one sense we are never free because we cannot refuse our necessities. If we could, they would be possibilities but not requirements, and here I am concerned solely with the inescapable demands and restrictions that are strictly necessary. These we can master only if we are in the service of a kingly lord: an end so extensive and substantial that we can bring even the most burdensome imperatives under his dominion, and thereby align our necessities so that they minister to us in serving him. By accepting that one authority over ourselves, we achieve authority over all the rest. Because we are bound, we are free.

So it was through my love and marriage, and the discovery of my theological vocation, that I learned how faith and freedom are one reality seen from different directions. My first and final freedom was the freedom to choose my lord. Even in the compelling transports of unitive belief, I had been free to commit myself to what was given me there, or to count it among my pleasant but intrinsically meaningless experiences. Nevertheless, I was free only to the degree that I gave my trust and consented to be carried. Having faith, I had a basis for theologizing, for responding to life, for living, as physically I could walk from place to place because the ground supported me, or as an airplane can fly because the density of the air in relation to its speed resists its falling: it could not fly at all in a vacuum. Like the plane, I would fall if my speed diminished, if I did not exercise my freedom by growing but tried to live by a static object of belief instead of the movement from faith to faith.

And I did fall, very soon, away from nearly everything I had learned since I first asked why I should live, and back into the state of mind that had dominated my childhood. I had left it behind, but it did not leave me because I had never plainly faced it and resolved my differences with it.

5. *The Demand for Righteousness*

"It" or "he." This was the last hair that I split during the momentous period between my graduation from college and my establishment as a wife. It was also the subject on which Emerson and I had our first serious quarrel. Is the Christian's authority an "it" or a "thou"? Is Christianity to be defined by obedience to Jesus' teaching, or by accepting him as Lord? No dispute over money, or individual rights and responsibilities in marriage, or any of the other more traditional issues that end a honeymoon, could have been fiercer or more anguished for us both.

I took the ancient and honorable position that the heart of the Christian faith is a principle, an "it". As Dr. H. B. Sharman once said, "You can start with ethics. In fact, what is God but ethics? What is God but the demand for righteousness, man's confrontation with the totality of good?" Emerson defended the equally ancient and honorable position that the person of Jesus was the way, the truth, and the life, and that his teaching was incidental to what he was. We agreed on the prime requirement for the Christian of obedience, of submission to a power outside of and greater than ourselves. Long before, and separately, we had concluded that an external authority was indispensable for any stability in thought or action. But is that final authority a principle or a person? Does the Christian obey a law or a master? And what difference does it make which he chooses?

Historically, the evidence appears to be conclusive: the main stream of Christian doctrine flows in the channel of loyalty to a person, although the currents of adherence to a principle are also strong. Knowing very little of Christian history, I did not argue with Emerson on that ground, but confined myself to the insistence that on this point, the fathers of the church and their successors were wrong. My husband replied that perhaps they were, and perhaps they entirely misunderstood Jesus' life and message, but Christianity could only be defined historically, so if I interpreted the Gospel in some other way, I might be right but I was not Christian.

In an access of perversity, I wanted to be both right and Christian. In other words, I wanted Christianity to stand for what I believed was true, particularly my conviction that the good life consists in conforming inwardly and outwardly to the implacable demand for righteousness. I admitted that the standards imposed by "the totality of good" were not easy to discern, but I was certain that they would become progressively clearer as my meticulous obedience to what I could perceive now would form me more closely according to its pattern. Life was a matter of adjusting myself to an unchanging and unchangeable Law, or of being destroyed by it if I failed in my comprehension and duty.

It is up to scholars to determine whether the legalistic strain in Christianity is central or peripheral to that faith. Many revered authorities are to be found on both sides. The question remains whether it represents a true or false picture of human nature, because it is perfectly possible for a belief to be true but not Christian. Having lived by such a legalism persistently and (I think) intelligently for a number of years — it was the mood which dominated my childhood and I am still not entirely free from it — I am now convinced that Christian or not, it is devastatingly false in theory and injurious in practice.

If in the end the order in the universe is the manifestation of an impersonal principle or law or force or entity, whether of righteousness, love, or anything else, the attempt to live by it will ultimately destroy the person as a person. He will turn into a thing — a thinking, a human animal, perhaps, but not a person. The warning that we become like what we worship is truer than is usually recognized. So in relating myself to an impersonal law, I tended to take on its impersonality. I judged myself in terms of my success or failure in adapting myself to something that could react to me as an entity but could not respond to me as a person, and would not if it could. It was everything to me; I was nothing to it except a potential tool, valuable — if at all — for my usefulness in performing good acts and inwardly shaping my thoughts and desires so as to perform better ones.

"Goodness" was indeed richly inclusive. Music was good because it refreshed the person who loved it; friendship was good because it manifested a moral achievement; even the detective stories to which I was (and am) addicted served the excellent purpose of temporarily detaching me from my immediate problems, enabling me to return to them with a better perspective. My prayers for help and my sense of being carried were forgotten. Now, when I prayed, it was that the power of righteousness would fit me for its service. All problems became ethical. All behavior was to be judged for its moral quality. The experience of unitive faith would return when I had earned it.

I did not, I could not live consistently by this theology, although God knows that I tried to, and condemned myself severely for my daily lapses. For one thing, often the demand for righteousness seemed not to be applicable. I could find no way of relating it to the grave difficulties that Emerson and I ran into because of our extreme differences in temperament and background, or to the heart-breaking and heart-lifting vicissitudes of parish life where usually the most pressing issues could not be defined in terms of right and wrong, or even of good, better, and best. The attempt to do so was like trying to measure temperature with a yardstick. For another, even when the "good" in a given situation was clear in the abstract, often it could not be implemented, although to neglect it was against conscience and reason alike.

To give only one example, there was the church to which Emerson was called for the stated task of winning the young people to become active in it, although — as we learned too late — the church leaders restricted him to the methods that had already driven them out: discussion groups for youngsters who were already finding their pleasure in the local dance hall, protracted choir rehearsals for adolescents who wanted to date. We could not meet their needs without offending, if not actually injuring, the older people whose needs for social stability and emotional reassurance were equally acute, but so unlike their children's needs that neither group could be brought to see the other side of the problem.

The conflict here was not fundamentally a matter of different moralities, although it had drastic moral consequences. It was between different theologies, world views, and therefore could not be reached by moral arguments. A warped morality cannot be changed by the simple inculcation of higher moral principles, because morality grows out of theology. Our understanding of the nature of the world and man determines what we shall believe to be good and evil. No direct attack upon ethical standards could be successful with, for instance, people who were genuinely convinced that swearing is as great an evil as war, that incest is less reprehensible than smoking cigarettes, and that all members of churches using wine for communion are *ipso facto* drunkards. And these are actual, not fabricated, illustrations.

Within culturally isolated communities such as those, rule by impersonal law is practicable if all their members are committed to the same law, so that the inevitable discords can be resolved by referring to a mutually acceptable authority. In the three churches we served, there had been no agreement upon standards for half a generation or more. Only in the structure of the problem did the factions see eye to eye, and myself with them. We believed that the Christian life consisted in adjusting oneself to an absolute ethical demand. We conceived its content variously, but the structure of the pattern — a fixed law to which one forced himself to conform — was identical.

Although outward behavior can be forced, often without special trouble or damage, what we were striving for was an inner adaptation, a transformation of our inner selves. To do good was not enough for us; we required ourselves to be good. So we struggled to bring ourselves into line with the laws of love and righteousness that we worshipped, and some of us succeeded: those (I think now) who were blessed with a gracious and gentle disposition to begin with, and were fortunately situated in a social milieu which placed no severe strains on their graciousness and gentleness. Others, by unremitting self-discipline, concealed or destroyed their impulses toward forbidden ways of life. Constructing a straitjacket for their personal selves, they wrested a blessing from the community while they lived in hidden torment. But I, along with a few others, was equipped with a passionate and rebellious temperament that could not be regulated in that way, and surroundings where any passion or rebellion, for or against anything, was taken as clear evidence of ungodliness. The watchword in those communities was peace with God and one's fellows, by which was meant an almost superhuman — or inhuman — stoicism.

Splitting the hair between "he" and "it", I chose wrongly, and it took me years to learn the simple fact that the attempt to recreate myself in an impersonal image was both futile and evil, even though it was an image I had chosen for myself. When finally a psychiatrist pointed out in so many words that I had tried to fit myself into a mold wholly unsuited to me, I laughed aloud — the healing laughter of recognizing how ridiculous I had been: a mountain stream trying to make myself a tranquil lake, a gaudy sunflower thinking it could turn itself into a dignified rose. A myriad of experiences and observations had prepared me for his admonition: the story of the ugly duckling had been my favorite fairy story from the time I was a child. Now it came home to me like a revelation, and with manifest joy I took another step: changes in persons are not brought about by direct efforts to change them.

We are what we are, whether we like ourselves or not. We cannot force ourselves into a pattern, even one of our own devising. Any theology that calls for our adjusting ourselves to an impersonal standard of righteousness or love or humanitarianism or anything else, is a bad theology because it runs counter to the salient facts of human personhood, notably that our intrinsic selves are not under our direct control so that to tamper with them invariably leads to disaster. I had been trying to shape my spontaneous reactions into harmony with what I believed they ought to be, to feel the emotion of affection toward congregations who rejected me and the world out of which I came, to cherish values I could not share, to be the kind of wife that I thought my husband ought to have. With laudable intentions and lamentable sense, I had fallen victim to the belief that I knew what kind of person I ought to become, and that I could choose what kind of person it was possible and right for me to become.

In my experience of myself and observation of others, I have found that belief to be unmitigated nonsense, an illusion rooted in pride and flowering in the disease that is currently called alienation. It may be, as the myth in Genesis suggests, that man has authority to name, and by implication to define and control, all that exists around him. But our own names and definitions we cannot choose — as even in the beginning, according to the biblical story, Adam and Eve did not name themselves: God named them. What we do with what we are is up to us, but we cannot decide for ourselves what we are, and we become free in ourselves only when we accept the names — which is to say, the natures — we have been given, and thereby become willing to be ourselves, and finally will to be our own selves. Even after my brief psychiatric counseling, I still preferred another name and function, and admired other definitions more than my own. But at least I no longer rebelled against my necessity, and for the moment I was flooded with the joyous relief of knowing that I was not required to make myself anew.

Two consequences immediately followed that illumination. First, I began the long process of training myself to look outward in order to see what in the world needed to be done that I could do, instead of looking inward to find out who I was. Second, by and large I stopped worrying about the demand for righteousness. I did not sit down and figure out that an impersonal law is an inappropriate focus for a personal commitment. Quite simply, as time went on its challenge no longer challenged me. Neither did I work systematically through the alternatives, to reach the conclusion that if the ultimate authority were not impersonal, it must be in some sense personal. In so far as I thought about it at all, I felt that the hypothesis of a personal God was too naïve for my sophisticated tastes, too primitive for my educated intellect, and too closely associated with fundamentalistic literalism for my generally liberal theology.

For a decade or so I stood between two worlds and two selves — one humanistic, the other theistic — one dying, the other just beginning its struggle to be born. My central problem was still that of authority. What in the world or out of it could I trust to support and direct me? How could any authority be tested? What standards could I use for a judgment between competing authorities? What could I hold as true? Those questions were not answered until I brought into my theological structure something that had happened to me before I asked, "Why live?" and even before the outrage of surgery, but to which I had not for many years given serious consideration: a dream.

chapter four

THE PLACE OF THE DREAM

> 'Day unto day uttereth speech ...'
> What if
> the whole night spoke?
> what if the cyclic stars forsook
> their serene orbits? broke
> that order which is heaven's first law? what if
> they moved, regrouped themselves, and wrote,
> gigantic on the dark above my head,
> some dread
> intelligible word?
>   J. REDWOOD ANDERSON, *Transvaluations*

1. *The Dream*

The dream occurred in the early morning of July 22, 1933. I was sixteen years old.

I was crossing a desert of red sand and red rocks, under a red sky. The footing must have been rough because I remember my relief at a moment's rest when I came to a comparatively clear space. Although I could not see anyone else, I knew that around me others were trudging in the same direction. Where we were going, why we were there, I did not know. In silence we simply plodded on.

After a time, I was on the ledge of a cliff overlooking the red plain. I could see — not see, but sense — those others more distinctly. Something that was, or that carried, a visible flame went from one to another but not to all. It seemed to pick an erratic course among them. And I knew that it was coming next to me.

I waited for it because there was nothing else I could do. Even if I had not been paralyzed by terror, there was no place on that narrow ledge for me to go. It approached. It reached me and I was swept by an intense heat that burned me without pain. It engulfed me for a period that cannot be measured because it was not a period of time. I endured it in that eternity which is without beginning or end or duration. Simultaneously, I was utterly annihilated and utterly fulfilled beyond any possibility of description. When it had gone, I held gold in my hand.

I woke speaking words that had been given me: "Gold from dross."

* * * * * *

Was it a dream or a vision? Was it the product of psychological tensions deep in my subconscious, or a revelation from God? In college, when I came across the writings of the mystics, I recognized instantly that my dream differed from the classic mystical experience only in that it had occurred, or had begun, when I was asleep. Substantially and existentially they were identical. But the same questions have to be asked of the indubitable mystics. Psychological state or divine revelation? Dream or vision?

The arguments in favor of its being a dream are impressive. As Dr. MacLeod informed me when I told him about it, such dreams are not at all uncommon during adolescence. They belong to a general type which has been widely investigated and is now well enough understood that any reasonably competent psychologist or psychiatrist can easily trace those phenomena to their source in sexuality or racial memory or whatever. The psychological or psychiatric manner of handling the event, however, leaves open a series of important questions. Does their explanation not commit the genetic fallacy? While the psychological history of a dream may totally account for its occurrence, does its origin explicate the whole range of its significance and meaning? Can the root explain the flower? Is the whole equivalent to the sum of its parts, and can the whole be comprehended by analyzing it into its parts? Does the initial step determine the entire course of the journey?

I had been well trained in the principles of dynamic interaction of parts within a whole, so that every part acquires its meaning, and in a real sense its identity, by its participation within the whole. Thus I was prepared for two distinct and irreconcilable interpretations of the dream. Either the sexual impulse (or other psychological event) constituted the frame of reference that would elucidate the dream, or the dream provided the frame of reference by which sexuality (or whatever) should be interpreted. If the governing principle were psychological, the inclination to center my attention on the dream itself was presumably a defense mechanism enabling me to rationalize my repressions. If the dream were the governing principle, my sexuality must be understood in the terms supplied by the dream.

In the dream, I had felt as if I were being approached by something beyond and alien to myself, an Other. Psychologists could give a coherent and persuasive explanation of it. The explanation of the mystics was equally coherent and persuasive. The alternatives implied different doctrines of man and carried different consequences for living, but I could not generate much concern over those implications. Through the years I was drawn down and down to the one point: what had come to me in the dream — God or my unconscious self? Had I been confronted with something outside or inside myself? And how, in heaven's name, could I tell? On what ground could I make such a determination?

Although I finally decided that it was God who had met me there, I did not choose that alternative because it solved more of my problems. If anything, it raised more since it set me in opposition to the general world view and mood of the world in which I had been brought up and which still surrounded me. Not because it offered a simpler rationale for living. On the contrary, by isolating me from my fellows, it created complications of many kinds. Not because it saved me from the judgment that my innermost self was a sink-hole and my actions the result of despicable motives. If the dream were from a God, his judgment — as expressed in the annihilative aspect of the dream — was even more terrible. Instead, my choice was made on the only ground which in the end can be held and defended with complete integrity: that one alternative rang true, and the other did not. Bluntly, I made my choice on the basis of personal preference.

I do not know of any basis for choice which is as disreputable as personal preference — meaning by disreputable "of bad repu-

71

tation," whether the reputation is deserved or not. The dictum, "I prefer it," is usually thought of as the last, infuriating refuge of those who obstinately and arbitrarily refuse to think. And so it sometimes is. But it can also be the final affirmation of insight and responsibility. To prefer is not an act of the intellect alone or of the will alone, or even the acquiescence to an emotion. It is instead an act of the person functioning integrally. Thus I could not take a stand based upon reason, because reason demonstrated the validity and cogency of both positions. I could not follow my desires because they were confused. I could not will because I did not know what to will. The parts of myself, separated, impelled me in many directions when what I needed was one direction. The best I could do, therefore, was to clarify all these (and other) factors as much as possible and then compare the finished structures, not item by item but in their total impact upon me and my total response to them.

The act of preferring cannot be analyzed into component elements any more than life can be studied in a dismembered body. To prefer is to declare one's integrity, to be — at least for the moment — integrated, whereas analysis destroys the integrity that it studies. At the beginning of the process of determining what the dream should mean, I had not had integrity because I did not know which of the alternatives I preferred, which meant that I did not know who I was. More accurately, I knew that I was disintegrated, a double self who was simultaneously attracted both to the pellucid categories and procedures of psychology, and to the vastness and abounding vitality of the theological enterprise. I could not follow both ways at once. I must choose between viewing theology from the standpoint of psychology, or psychology from the standpoint of theology. I could not give my heart to one and my head to the other, or leap back and forth between them with no place to rest. All of myself was involved; therefore all of myself must decide, and in some fashion other than by splitting myself in pieces and tabulating the votes from the fragments.

The discovery of my preference meant what might be called my official determination to develop according to one particular pattern and not the other. Looking back, I do not see how I could have chosen otherwise without violating what is most characteristically my personal identity. If I had fixed on psychology, sooner or later I would surely have broken the pattern of professional detachment as I did break the pattern of "the minister's wife". It seems as if I had no real freedom there, because a person cannot maintain a preference against his intrinsic nature. But the person looking back is the person who was, if not created by that decision, at least liberated by it. After the decision had been made (over a period of years, not in a moment as this narrative might suggest), it appeared to have been foreordained. Before it was made, I knew beyond any question that I was authentically free to move in any of several directions.

There is no contradiction between my description of preference and my earlier assertion that we cannot directly change ourselves or determine directly whom we will become. Here I was not operating directly upon myself, attempting to excise undesirable impulses or to poultice frustrations or to modify posture with a self-imposed brace. My attention was focussed on the metaphysical problem, "What kind of a world is this?" — a world where the dream represented a domestic explosion or where it resulted from a foreign invasion? I was examining the dream for its nature and meaning, concentrating upon something outside my own self, and I discovered and directed that self in the only way that is appropriate to its nature or that can be effective: indirectly and incidentally.

We are all continually under pressure to alter our understanding of the world, our metaphysics, world view, theology. Whatever our preference of yesterday, made in terms of yesterday's intentions, feelings, information, and outward circumstances, today we know more and may be feeling and planning differently, or living in a different world. Daily we reaffirm or disavow yesterday's preference. No position is necessarily final. So, for example, less than a year after my dream occurred, in effect I renounced the world view it implied when at the time of my appendectomy, I failed to grasp the connection between those two events: that before I was lacerated by the outrage, the glory had supplied the means for healing the wound because the glory, where annihilation and fulfilment were inconceivably one, included the outrage while the outrage forever excluded the glory.

I apostasized from the dream a second time when I accepted the psychological interpretation as fully adequate, and a third time, when having sworn fealty to the dream as revelation, I neglected to trace out and act upon the practical implications of my choice. For most purposes, I forgot about it and it remained on the periphery of my conscious theology for several years. It was another several years before it gradually made its way to the region close to the heart of my thought, and it is entirely possible that someday it will be back on the periphery again.

Still, I had entered paradise as a guest, and even through the period when I affirmed the dream as a vision but disregarded it, the desire remained to become a citizen of the paradisal state. And how could I not desire it, who had once seen the glory unveiled in a dream, and had lived the glory for a moment at once in and out of time?

The question is not rhetorical. It was not inevitable that I should have sought a return to the paradise of the vision-dream. I was not compelled either theologically or psychologically. Others have dreamed such dreams and have written the experience off as a trifling episode, delightful but without determinative meaning. I had come very close to it myself. I had almost denied its reality and significance, and settled myself to attain pleasure in living instead of the rending joy of heaven, success instead of fulfilment. Only by a shred, a whisper, the splitting of a hair, had I saved the dream from oblivion. Here also I was not a passive victim of social forces or a puppet of God. I chose, and I was responsible for my choice.

I believe now that the dream made the decision peculiarly difficult. It was an extreme experience, and the farther an event departs from the commonplace, the stronger our temptation to consider it abnormal, a symptom of a pathological condition. It is easier to believe something that is less dramatic and less at odds with ordinary life, just as it is easier to learn a language that is closely related to our native tongue than one which stems from an entirely different root.

2. *The Imaginative Function*

Theologically, one of the most interesting features of the dream is that it contributed to my thinking an image rather than a rational concept or a religious doctrine. Like a story, a picture, a dance, it appealed to my imagination rather than to my intellect, and therefore communicated more than it explicitly said.

A rational concept or doctrine or idea can be conveyed from intellect to intellect without fundamentally changing, within the limits of approximately equal competence and training: the periodic table of elements has essentially the same meaning for all chemists. But images speak to the whole person in all his complexity as a particular historical being. They are connotative rather than denotative. Great music does not explain: it evokes. The great myths are not diagrams of truth: they display truth in action. A great painting does not stimulate the discursive reason: it enriches the self. The meaning of an image depends as much upon how and by whom it is received as upon what it is in itself. It is verified not by objective evidence or rational demonstration, but by its power to seize our imaginations. And its freight is transmitted by non-rational means, often by the arts.

"The chief difficulty of living," writes Charles Morgan, "is the difficulty we all have in perceiving what the form of our life really is or indeed that it has a form." It is the sense of form which art contributes to the theological enterprise, by presenting us with images in endless diversity and leaving us free to respond in our own individual ways. Some works of art leave us untouched. Others repel us. Still others, however, speak forcibly to our condition by nourishing, healing, and enchanting us. We do not impregnate them with meaning and power; they impregnate us. So we find ourselves turning repeatedly to this novel or that symphony, perhaps knowing that by critical standards they are not "great" productions, but not caring because they satisfy a hunger in us that is otherwise unfulfilled, or awake a capacity that otherwise sleeps, or restore clarity to eyes that are otherwise dulled.

These particular creations may not have any such effect on anyone else in the world. The artist may have had no such intention when he created them. In any case, whatever art is or should be, its essential function is not to serve theological or religious ends, even though incidentally it may have implications for theology and religion. Any theological consequences of art should not be in the form of displaying an idea or system, much less with the purpose of persuading us that one belief is true and others false, one good and others evil. What great art does is to enable us to imagine for ourselves, and thereby to develop our own sense of form. Then, if we choose, we can distill concepts from our images, and diagram the forms we have imagined to produce theological systems. But it is the images that generate the ideas, and ideas — concepts, principles, abstractions — become meaningful and productive only to the degree that we image the realities to which they refer.

The dependence of ideas upon images can be illustrated by the current status of the doctrine that the Christian God is transcendent. The very idea of transcendence, certain theologians tell us, has become empty of all meaning. For many persons, the word now is no more than a set of nonsense syllables. While I agree with the observation I do not agree with the reasons usually given to explain it: that our scientifically oriented world view excludes any such possibility as that of a transcendent realm or being; that reliance upon such an external referent is unnecessary or pernicious; or that the primitive impulses which originally produced the doctrine have been outgrown by our sophisticated culture.

My own explanation is simpler: that "modern man" cannot think about or believe in a transcendent God because since early childhood, his imagination has been neither exercised nor disciplined, until now it is partially paralyzed. Because we have been forbidden to imagine other worlds than the "naturalistic" or "scientific" except as a frivolous pastime, our concept of transcendence has no roots in imagery and no imaginative vitality. Neither have many other of the enriching and quickening ideas of the past. In effect, we have castrated our intellects by severing them from the personal functions of imagining, feeling, intuiting, adoring, and therefore from the wealth and energy of our subconscious lives. While we are thus able to think more and more precisely, our thoughts have less and less substance. Although we have become increasingly skilled in relating concepts to each other, we are increasingly clumsy in relating any concept meaningfully to our actual existence. The gains in precision and clarity have been won at the cost of fertility and relevance.

I first became conscious of the pressures that vitiate the imagination when I must have been somewhere around six or seven years old. A visitor in our home, a family friend who was also a child psychologist, amused himself (or so I remember his attitude) one afternoon while he was waiting for my parents, by asking me if I believed in fairies. I was quite old enough to understand that the correct answer for a person of my age and intelligence, was No, and that Yes would shamefully brand me as still a baby. However, I could not honestly answer either Yes or No, because I both did and did not believe in fairies, and the words and concepts at my command were not adequate to define the critical distinction between fairies as creatures, whom I did not really believe in, and the realm of faërie, which represented something very deep and vulnerable and dear that I did believe in. If I said Yes, I would betray this inmost faith to the psychologist, and almost certainly he would betray me to my parents and they to my sister and brother. But a No would be apostasy, cutting me off forever from participation in that realm. Feeling rather like a Joan of Arc choosing between recantation and the stake, I elected the stake, recognizing as I spoke the fateful Yes that it meant not assent to an intellectual thesis, but affirmation of loyalty to an image.

So far as I can recall, never until writing this section have I admitted to anybody that I believed in fairies or faërie. The world around me did not permit that kind of aberration. At the same time, the opinion of the world did not shake my secret loyalty. In nearly everything having to do with my imaginative life, I became both defensive and resolute to defend, and withdrew from the immediate battle to prepare my counterattack. Outwardly conforming, inwardly I followed my own way: feeding upon books that nourished my imagination, while justifying my preference to those around me on grounds that they would approve; writing what I called "poetry"; and breaking loose every now and then in ferocious tantrums. Later in my childhood, when I began to develop a sense of the holy that I somehow associated with the otherness of faërie, I hid that as well. These things were not supposed to be taken seriously because they could not be contained in words or arranged into any system that was acceptable to my associates. They were considered dangerous because they were alien to the officially recognized patterns of thought, and because by those canons they were wildly erratic in their effects.

It was obvious even to me, and even as a child and adolescent, that the imaginative functions can be misused. Without discipline, they produce unrealities and monstrosities: maundering reveries, waking nightmares, diseased fantasies, emotional and aesthetic chaos, intellectual and ethical decay. In the society that surrounded me in my early years, however, the prudence that ought to govern all imaginative activities had generally deteriorated into fear of the imagination as such. The adults around me, unable or unwilling to differentiate between a sterile fancy and a creative vision, urged me to pluck out my eyes in case they might offend me, thus saving me from the perils of sight but also ensuring that I should not receive its blessings.

The imaginative function cannot be destroyed easily, if at all, but it is remarkably easy to stupefy or pervert it. A little contemptuous laughter, a few gibes about enthusiasm, a supercilious remark or two about phases that will be outgrown, an occasional reference to symptoms of mental illness, will usually be quite enough to drive it underground where the images proliferate like a jungle or a malignancy, or fester, or decompose. Usually the best that the imaginative person can expect is to be left to learn for himself — and by himself — what the powers of imagination can and cannot be used for, and how they can be increased and controlled by intellectual and other disciplines.

Through such a process of obstinate, solitary, stumbling experimentation, I have formed the tentative conclusion that the primary, if not the sole, function of the rational mind is disciplinary, but that it must have something to discipline or it can do no more than refine the emptiness of formal diagrams. Rationality cannot go beyond itself into the realms of aesthetic and moral apprehension, religious celebration, and personal response. It cannot feed itself. The rational mind needs the imaginative functions to nourish it, and they need it to order them.

Between the sterility of the unimaginative intellect and the wanton fecundity of the undisciplined — or unwisely disciplined — imagination, there is not much to choose. Both are deadly. Their union in creativity, however, is a major achievement demanding all the resources of the person, as well as the courage to see with one's own eyes and to build with one's own hands. Since images, like emotions, are not under our direct control, we must not try to manipulate them forcibly or they will be destroyed. We must free them, and wait in patience for their birth and maturation according to the laws of their own nature. Our first principle in dealing with images must be openness, whether they are unspeakably dreadful or ineffably rapturous, highly structured or still amorphous. Initially we should not assess or direct them, but rather abandon ourselves that we may receive fully whatever they have to give.

The dream appears to reveal God? Faërie appears to be real? The beloved appears to comprise all beauty and goodness? The outrage discloses unconscionable depths of evil? The appearance may or may not reflect a reality, but in the beginning we are not concerned with reality at all. Our question is, "What does it seem to be, to us?" — because to paraphrase Charles Williams, a thing that seems has at least the truth of its seeming. It may have more; it cannot have less. "The eyes of Rosamond might or might not hold the secret origin of day and night, but if they apparently did, then they apparently did, and it would be silly to deny it and equally silly not to relish it." Our discipline at this point consists precisely in not judging and not interpreting, and especially in not imposing upon our images the interpretations of others. At another time our discipline will require us to examine the image intellectually, choosing which facets to emphasize and which to develop further, penetrating, clarifying, and finally ordering the relations of that image with others. But the first act is that of receptivity, and it is this action which is discouraged if not forbidden by our educational theories and social institutions.

It is characteristic of images that they perform most of their functions in secret. We may be aware of the moment when they invade us, but the manner of their growth is usually hidden, and the ways and degrees of their influence upon our other images, as well as upon our rational concepts, are scarcely perceptible until their principal work is done. They pierce those levels that are deeper than our conscious minds, where creative activity takes place. We do not know what is happening there until a work of art, an intuition, a fresh idea reaches full term and is born into consciousness. By taking thought, we can change our ideas. Our attitudes and impulses, however, are changed only by the power of the imagination as one image displaces another by processes that we cannot yet analyze and can rarely, if ever, observe.

Therefore I cannot trace the chronological sequence of my theological development from the time when I dismissed the dream from conscious consideration to the time when I realized

that it and the image of faërie were silently but decisively altering the foundations of my living — not only my world view,
but also my spontaneous reactions. I did not wake up one
morning to find that my world view had changed. Gradually,
in the years that followed my reacceptance of them, I found as
I worked through problem after problem that with increasing
frequency and urgency, I was asking myself whether this or
that idea, image, or response was compatible with accepting the
dream and faërie as valid images.

I do not consider my childish belief in faërie as having been
a precondition for my adult perception of transcendent holiness.
Undoubtedly the imaginative function is such a precondition,
because we cannot move from ideas and sense perceptions to
anything beyond them except as imagination pierces the shell
of the obvious and the customary, fertilizing not only our intellects but ourselves. We can barricade ourselves against its
invasions and so become stunted creatures who inhabit a progressively hardening and dwindling world. Or we can welcome
it as an enlargement and enablement of mind and self. Both
acceptance and rejection of imagery are dangerous. If we set
a priori limits on the imagination, censoring what images we
shall and shall not receive, we shut ourselves up within self-
constructed boundaries and our world will never become larger
than it is now. Yet if we submit to invasion by images, we
cannot predetermine what or whom shall penetrate us, much
less whether it will belong to our orders of magnitude and kind,
or be something to which we can appropriately give the name
"revelation."

3. *The Revelatory Function*

Logically, although not chronologically, my doctrine of revelation grows out of the observation that while I bestow meanings on things and persons around me, the dream bestowed
meaning on me. I am caught within a process of giving and
receiving meanings that can be illustrated most clearly by the
development of very young children. A tiny baby will alternate
between spontaneous expressions of preference, so rudimentary
as scarcely to deserve the name, and accommodation to what
goes on around it. At one moment it "prefers" to eat, at another
to sleep. It asserts its own nature. But the infant soon learns
that certain movements or sounds or touches signify the advent

of satisfactions, or frustrations. Rejoicing or protesting, he submits to persons and things which assert their own natures against his. As the reciprocal interaction between liberty and restraint, self-assertion and acquiescence, becomes more sophisticated, he develops a sense of his own identity, his own meaning.

To a great extent, the child appropriates his definitions of the world and himself from those who function *in loco parentis* to him. They teach him meanings which he accepts for a time. Sooner or later, however, he is likely to revolt against whatever meaning they have given him, and apply to himself a meaning of his own choice, occasionally expressed with delightful precision by his insistence upon calling himself — and requiring that others call him — by a name that he himself has selected. The interplay goes on (or should go on) all our lives. We impose meanings on the world, and meanings are imposed upon us. We assert our authority over things and persons, including ourselves, by assigning meanings to them; and we yield to authorities who effectually designate meanings for us.

The functional difference between giving and receiving meanings provides the basis for my definition of a "natural theology" as a world view that sets forth the meanings we give to things, as contrasted to a "revealed theology" that sets forth the meanings we have received from sources outside ourselves. Thus in my vocabulary, "nature" and "revelation" do not refer to fixed essential qualities, but to the functional relationship between ourselves and that which surrounds us. What ultimately determines the natural or revelatory function of an event is our response to it. It follows that what for one person is an authentic revelation may be natural or meaningless to another, and that contradictory revelations are not only possible but inevitable. More important, it follows that revelations can be "naturalized," and events that originally were "natural" can become "revelations".

For example, when I was small, my parents taught me that I was a child of God. They revealed to me something about my place and significance in the universe that conceivably I might have worked out for myself, but in fact did not. According to my terminology, this was a revelation in the full sense of the word: a meaning which I received from a source outside myself. As I absorbed that meaning, however, complacency replaced wonder. Claiming the gift as a right, I defined myself as a child of God and so naturalized the revelation. The revelation first changed me, and then I changed it. Consequently, the pattern of expectations which then constituted my world view altered from a revealed to a natural pattern.

When the dream occurred, it shattered my view of myself and the world by revealing a totally new range of meanings. Before I had time to naturalize the dream to any profound extent, the revelation of the outrage gave me still another meaning, and I defined myself in terms of that horror. The dream, therefore, was first a revelation and then a natural event, and eventually it became a revelation again when I restored it to its original function as that which gave meaning to me.

Each wave of the process begins when we receive a meaning for ourselves, and ends when we appropriate that meaning by giving it to ourselves. As the revelation becomes the basis for a new theology, its revelatory function is transformed into a natural function, and the revealed theology into a natural theology that — naturally — resists further encroachments by further revelations. For this reason, if I had not been persuaded that I was the child of a loving God, the outrage would have been far less damaging. Because of my approximately Christian upbringing, I already possessed the "truth" that God is love and I am his child, and it was "truth for me". So paradoxically, I was at once dreadfully vulnerable to the shocks of living, and dreadfully armored against creative response to such shocks. How could there be a further or different revelation? Therefore, when my natural theology was stripped from me by the outrage, I was lamentably defenseless.

I would have been equally defenseless, however, with any other natural theology, including a more adequate comprehension of what Christianity means by "God" and "a child of God". No matter how sublime the patterns, their breaking and the subsequent restructuring of the person are requisites for growth, and can be avoided only by dying the death of refusing to grow. Often, certainly, I have resisted growth. I have wanted an improved version of what I already had rather than the earthquake that left me stunned and disorganized. But a major revelation is a shaking of the foundation, and even a minor one — a bit of gossip that wounds our pride — will weaken it if only by a hairline crack. Because natural theologies are our own creations, always they concur with our inclinations. Because the revelations come from outside ourselves, always they demolish our calculations or subvert our pleasures, and so we find them hard to comprehend and absorb.

It is natural, for instance, to suppose that a good God will harken to good people and place them under his special protection. That is the way we naturally behave with people whom we approve and like. But it is not natural — it is likely to be a startling and repugnant revelation — to suppose that a good God will lavish upon evil persons the same loving concern that he pours out upon those who are worthy of it. Neither the consciously good nor the consciously evil person finds this easy to believe because it offends the sense of impartial justice in both. Conversely, a revelation may be incredible because it seems too joyous, too good to be true. It may impart an abundance of life that we had not dreamed of possessing, and we resist it not from abhorrence but from fear of later disappointment.

Since revealed theologies inevitably conflict with natural theologies, a natural theology cannot develop smoothly or directly into a revealed theology. By a leap of faith, we can travel farther along a road we have already mapped out, but we are not transported into a new country because the leaping is something that we do, not something that is done to us. On the other hand, natural theologies can block revelations by hardening our hearts, freezing our imaginations, and decisively closing our minds.

Our natural theologies are always wrong. Always they are incomplete or disproportioned or imprecise, if not positively in error. Yet it is right to build them. Each of them constitutes a step on the way to brighter illumination, and they are necessary steps. Until the first lesson has been mastered, the first revelation assimilated, the second cannot be grasped. The second must be appropriated before we can receive the third. Our real dangers lie in failing to embrace our successive revelations. As Charles Williams once wrote, "Unless devotion is given to a thing which must prove false in the end, the thing that is true in the end cannot enter." Unless we worship the highest that we can see, we shall not be ready for the invasion of something higher still. If we refrain from adoration until we are sure of having an object worthy of our homage, our capacity to adore will wither. But we do not need to enshrine our preparatory images as definitive idols. We look at an idol for itself, but through an image to something beyond it. Idols paralyze the imagination while images empower it. Idolatry is static, imagery a driving force toward renewal of life and therefore toward the death which is the precondition for renewal.

I am participating in a historical process that has its own rhythm of speed and rest, its own methods of progression, its own purpose and goal, and I know it only as I can. At first, my ability to see the process was severely limited, but the revelation of parental authority prepared me to recognize more extensive and weightier authorities; the worship of images trained me in the elementary skills and arts of worship; my little deaths are equipping me for my final dying. As long as I apprehend these stages as constituting an integral process of alternate building and breaking, all is well. It is when I interpret any stage as a terminus that I become diseased. And when I scheme to control the rhythm and design, I become perverted.

What I do is of nature. What is done to me, through whatever medium, is revelatory: an impregnation from a world beyond myself. Sun, moon, and stars; animal, vegetable, and mineral; lover, friend, and foe: they are all visitations from outside the confines of my self, revealing the existence of an other that resists me and therefore can support me. To the degree that I give meaning to the other and others, they are natural phenomena. To the degree that they give meaning to me, they are not natural but supernatural: diabolic or divine.

Therefore it was good for me to have been taught that God is my father. Nothing better could have been revealed to me. I could have done nothing better than to have naturalized that revelation. And nothing better could have happened than to have the revelation destroyed. Because my rigidity made me vulnerable, I was overthrown, and because I was shattered too radically to rebuild myself in my own image, I was able to accept another revelation. By assimilating the glory, I corrupted it, and the corruption prepared me for another access of the glory. I created a theology and it was destroyed so as by fire. In the ruins I built a better structure, thereby inviting a more pervasive holocaust. What I now heartily believe will no doubt someday be overthrown, and in renewed agony of mind, spirit, and body I shall have to build again. But there is no alternative except to refuse the fire of my dream which obliterates what it fulfils and fulfils what it obliterates in a consummation beyond words, thoughts, and images. "He that seeketh to gain his life shall lose it, and he that loseth his life shall find it."

4. *The Function of the Body*

Through all these vicissitudes, one thing has remained relatively constant: my physical body and everything for which the body is the vehicle and symbol. My ancestors live on in me. I did not choose them, nor did they choose me, but their genes established my potentialities and limitations, and their behavior in a long chain of influences affected my distant forebears, my parents, and me. They created the governments and cultures that determine the kind of society I am living in. Though I may sometimes denounce them, I am derived from them and to some degree their lives are justified or not justified by mine. I am not under any obligation to be grateful for their contributions to me, but ordinary honesty compels me to acknowledge the fact of my derivation from them and its implications, notably that I am rooted in the past. I not only live in history but I have a history, and so long as I am embodied I carry that history within the very cells of my bones and my blood.

The two supreme gifts of my body to my self are continuity and integrity. Indeed the body changes, although more sluggishly than the mercurial intellect and emotions, and less radically. It is bound by its physiological requirements into the seamless fabric of the universe. It must have food, water, and air in order to survive, and is shamelessly dependent upon other beings for them. Our bodies, as much as our minds, hunger for companionship, for the touch that at once assures us that we are not alone and reassures us of our own identity in contrast with those others. In the harried interplay of modern life where frequently we must change our functions hourly — in swift succession be spouse, parent, child, superior, equal, subordinate, and must work, play, rest with little time for transition — it may be only the body that consistently vouches for our durable identity as selves. Again to quote Charles Williams: "All things are finally worked out in the body; all mysteries are there manifested, even if still as mysteries. It is the only crucible of the great experiment; its innocent, even if debased, purity endures the most difficult transmutations of the soul."

Times without number I have tried to disembody myself. When Emerson and I were married, we assured each other that we were not marrying our respective families; we were acting as individuals. But our families lived physically as well as mentally in us. When I was plagued with anxiety attacks, I believed that I could reason myself out of them, as if my body had no authority over my mind. When I saw a path of action clear before me, I did not expect that contrary impulses would frustrate my intentions, yet oppositions were continually springing from deep within me to counteract what I consciously wanted and willed. Whether these anxieties, impulses, legacies had specific physical origins does not matter here. They appeared to belong to me in the same way that my body does, and they rose up to confront me like elements of my own being, as surely though indescribably interior as my digestion and thoughts. Like the phenomena that are sometimes attributed to a racial memory, they may or may not be physiologically inherited, but they surge into consciousness as compulsions from within rather than as impositions from without. Like the body, they are experienced as having an inner source.

That which the body is, and carries, is irrational, childlike, primitive. By the standards of the rational mind, the contributions from the body are inexplicable and capricious. Naturally my sophisticated intellect resented such pressures against its authority, and as a civilized person I feared those relics of barbarism in myself and others. I have been right to fear them. They are daimonic, angelically or diabolically compelling, and therefore an imminent threat to self-determination. I have felt for most of my life that unless I conquered them, they would conquer me, and the last major theological step that I took before finishing this book was to discover that conquering and being conquered are not the only alternatives.

The occasion for that discovery was my slow recognition of the reason behind my dissatisfaction with the forms of public worship which are almost exclusively directed to the intellect and will through the ear and eye. After the outrage of surgery, I had grown away from the Episcopal Church in which I had been confirmed when I was 15, and just before our marriage, I had joined the Society of Friends. During most of the time since then, we lived in places where there were no Quaker meetings, so I participated with my husband in the Protestant Free Church tradition, as exemplified first in the Church of the Brethren of which his father had been a minister, and later the United

Church of Christ (Congregational), although I did not formally join either.

The time came, however, when the sermons, music, and fellowship of the Free Churches were not enough. I grew ravenous for touch and taste, for the satisfaction of a craving that is more visceral than cerebral or social or aesthetic or even imaginative, and is older in man than history or civilization. Childish it might very well be; very well, I would admit to being a child. For perhaps five years I consciously resisted the elemental impulses that were threatening what I felt was my adult dignity, my intellect openly fighting to retain the hegemony I had given it when I entered college. Thus it was with an acute sense of shame at losing my self-control that I finally asked for reinstatement in the Episcopal Church.

The defeat of my intellect on this point was not a victory for any dogma or institution. At the time I could go no farther than to say that I could no longer live satisfactorily without free access to the Eucharist. Subsequently it dawned on me that because the Eucharist is not merely a stimulus to thought but also a physical activity, and not merely a symbol but a rite that is enacted, it functions on a level of meaning that is not limited by consciousness. The eating of the consecrated bread and the drinking of the consecrated wine nourished both my physical body and the secret realms of the unconscious. The effect of consecration was not magical, automatically effective regardless of the recipient's knowledge or intention, like the repetition of a sorcerer's spell, but neither were knowledge and intention sufficient for its efficacy.

The mind can lay hold on the doctrine, which is the key that unlocks the door separating the unconscious from the conscious selves. But unlocking the door is not enough. The action is greater than the idea: because the rite is a physical act, it effectively opens the door, not necessarily bringing our hidden life into conscious awareness, but enabling each to impregnate the other in an interplay of complementary powers. Conscious life by itself is uninspired, pedestrian, conformist. Unconscious life by itself is savage, an unrestrained energy like primeval chaos, capable of almost any brutality or splendor. Wrongly joined, they are mutually destructive or self-abortive.

What my intellect had to surrender was not its authority but its autonomy, its claim to be independent of my visceral life.

The meeting of mind with mind had to be integrated — not balanced — with the significant touch of the hand, rational detachment with irrational celebration, civilized refinement with primitive vehemence, the adult with the child. Intellectual pride and personal self-respect struggled to preserve the supremacy of intellect and will over the primitive and unconscious self. Personal vitality, however, springs not from knowledge or volition but from the images that nourish our spirits, from the myths that incorporate our view of the world and ourselves, and from the rituals by which we join ourselves physically as well as mentally to the myths. And these images grow in the soil of our unconscious, not our conscious, lives.

The tribal legend, the professional "image", the hero and anti-hero, the sense of a "national destiny" or a religious fulfilment, all function as myths by serving as centers for a loyalty that is of the blood more than the brain. We adopt them because they gratify an inner need rather than a conscious ambition. The need may be good or evil, a healthy hunger or a pathological craving. So, for example, my image of self-control fed my ingrained pride, and fostered my communion with all those who believe that man's fate lies in his own enlightenment and self-determination. The proud man asserts, in whatever form, his self-possession. He rejects, in whatever degree, his dependence upon contingencies that are not subject to his will, as I rejected my dependence upon the visceral basis of human nature. Conversely, he may deny their dependence upon him: "What I do with my life is nobody's business except my own." Yet realistically, what each individual does and leaves undone determines what all his associates, from his immediate family to society as a whole, can and cannot do. To be proud is to live in the illusion of independence.

My return to the Episcopal Church, therefore, constituted the humiliating admission that I was not self-sufficient and that I could not control myself. So doing, I confessed that I was intellectually and morally incompetent to direct even my own affairs. I needed help of a kind that would thrust deeper than theological or psychological analysis to the dark places beyond speech and perception where the springs of life are concealed in the body. I dared not try to seek them out in order to identify their nature or analyze how they function, or to define how the bread and wine channeled them. There and at that time, it was enough that the sacramental act was effective, and because this was so, I conceded its authority to direct its own development.

For the moment, the probing, acquisitive mind to which nothing is — and nothing should be — sacred, was stilled. Temporarily I was content to accept rather than to seize: to eat and drink without asking how the process of digestion took place and without trying to anticipate the consequences. To describe my attitude as that of an observer is to dignify it more than it deserves. I was merely a recipient, passively obedient to the intuition that in the Eucharist something happens. What it was that happened, I did not know. Nor do I now when the intuition has grown into a conviction.

Although for several years I did not examine the nature and function of the Eucharist, my mind was active in more or less closely related areas, and occasionally would dart into an observation or hypothesis concerning it. I neither encouraged nor discouraged those ventures, which I suspected were indications that my mind was exploring new ways of functioning under the new régime where it was no longer the king of my little kingdom but a servant among servants, each with its special and irreplaceable function. Thus my problems with the primitive elements in myself changed from how to curb them by rationalization or forcible repression, to how I could express them appropriately. The problem of knowledge was no longer, "What is certainly true?" but the more modest, "How can the interrelationships of energies, entities, concepts, persons, be made productive?" As so often before, I did not work out in advance what form the new organization of myself should take. For that matter, I was not astute enough to expect that any serious changes in organization would follow. When I look back, I can see the process. At the time, I simply went where I felt impelled to go and trusted that illumination would finally be given me.

Unexpectedly, as my intellect defined and faced these new problems, it rejoiced and sang as if for the first time it had found its true vocation. It had never labored so strenuously. More was required of it than ever before because it could no longer restrict itself to the terms of its own choosing. It had to learn the subtler languages of aboriginal and visceral and spiritual response which are based on logical structures other than those of rationality. It had been well drilled in marching with other intelligences; now it started to dance with partners who were strange and wild.

I have often been astonished at the configurations of that dance, and occasionally troubled by misgivings when it led me farther from the march of contemporary thought than I felt safe in going. Meanwhile, I found companions whose writings encouraged and corrected me. We are not saying the same things or approaching our problems from the same direction, but we are alike in professing that man is the incarnation of daimonic principalities and powers as well as of rationality and self-determination, and that his consummation lies in their integration, not their separation or their balance. The unconscious daimons, like the physical body, are not in themselves angelic or devilish. What they become depends upon what or whom they serve.

Earlier I had given myself over to the service of righteousness and of rationality, both of whom become fiends when they are enthroned as deities. Now I found myself worshipping the God who is received in the Eucharist but is not contained in it, and who speaks a word that is not expressible in words. For the first or the fifth or the thirteenth time, I was becoming a convert to Christianity.

5. *"Why live?"*

The question that started me on my theological journey, "Why live?", had been as much visceral as cerebral, and therefore it could not be answered in cerebral terms alone. Because it had been a particular rather than a general question, it could not be adequately answered by a generalization, a doctrine, a principle. Theology — the intellectual and imaginative search for order in the world — was necessary but not enough. Ethics — the volitional and active response to the demand for righteousness — was also necessary but not enough. The element that had been lacking has several names; the one I prefer is "celebration", which includes not only worship but also the disposition to wonder that underlies worship, and much more than either of these. Celebration can be formal or informal, public or private, fiery or tranquil, jubilant or solemn, but whatever its occasion and form, it is an act involving all the unconscious energies which the body carries and contains, as well as the body itself, the imagination, the intellect, and moral determination.

The Place of the Dream

We can and should organize our experiences by formulating generalizations: scientific laws, ethical principles, philosophical abstractions, theological doctrines, aesthetic theories. By such processes of refining and synthesizing I had reached the general idea of a deity. But I do not live in a general world. I am not a person-in-general. I am a particular person living in a particular world and dealing with particular events. While I can think about and discuss a god-in-general, I can no more worship such a thing, or thank or berate or praise it, than I can cut down the abstract concept "tree" with a material axe or saw, or clear out an actual forest with images of tools. A god-in-general is too much of the remote mind, too little of the immediate, turbulent flesh, to serve as a focus for celebration. If the primal need to celebrate is met, its object will not be known initially through doctrines or arguments, and the doctrines and arguments will not be fully comprehended except through the act of celebrating.

What cannot be done by propositions can be done through stories. A story does not explain and a good story does not have a moral. Instead, it particularizes and so enlightens and enriches us particularly. The great stories speak to our changing conditions, impregnating us not at one stage only of our development but at many stages, progressively ordering both our conscious and unconscious lives, and continually animating our growth toward integrity.

I had deliberately used stories for this purpose at least from the time — when I was in high school, I think — that I first read G. K. Chesterton's *The Man Who Was Thursday,* and I continued to feed myself on stories for thirty years before I became theologically astute enough to understand why stories satisfied me in a way that other forms of communication did not. Novels, short stories, biographies and autobiographies, histories, legends, fantasies — any narrative would do so long as it quickened all levels of myself simultaneously with the sense, almost the touch, of particularity and integrity. Interestingly, the Bible has not done this for me except in two circumstances: my Old Testament classes at seminary under Prof. W. A. Irwin, and its liturgical use. As with Shakespeare's plays, I need to have those stories dramatized before they become alive and therefore revelatory. No doubt others persons function in other ways, but for me, the general idea is grasped through the particular, concrete image, and it requires both image and idea to release an effectual power.

A story can be told in many forms and interpreted in many ways. It is a center of reference rather than a limiting formula. It speaks to a variety of conditions, releasing the imagination rather than confining it. Thus when I employed philosophical and theological methods in my search for a principle of integration, I found a general deity, but when I celebrated the vision of integrity by means of stories and in the drama of the Eucharist, the God whom I found — or who revealed himself to me — was a particular God.

The only description of this particular God which I am willing to argue against all comers is that he opposes all my ideas about him, including the loftiest and including the idea that he opposes all my ideas. Whatever he may be, he is not restricted to what I think he is. My mind is too narrow to comprehend him, my life too meagre to receive him. Therefore I know him primarily, if not exclusively, as he interferes with me to my immense joy or inexpressible anguish. He is the Meddler, the Disrupter, the Opponent, the Invader, the Enemy, to such a degree that even the revelation of his love comes to me as a shock. I cannot envision of him, or of anything else in the universe, so exact and faithful a concern. When used of God, the word "love" expands its meaning until it no longer seems a fitting name for what I have known of him.

Against some comers, I am willing to argue that God is a person. I have found it useless to discuss the point at all with certain individuals to whom the notion of a personal responsiveness and communication is nonsense because the quality of "person" cannot be known by their techniques of impersonal investigation. By their standards, I cannot demonstrate that God exists at all, much less that he is a person, and my standards cannot be subsumed under theirs or translated into theirs.

The only definable ground I have for believing in a personal God is that at irregular intervals I have been summoned, stimulated, invaded, so intimately that I must either reject such experiences altogether or attribute them to a God who is a person. I cannot deny the reality and meaning of those encounters without denying my very existence as a person, because what they essentially do is to enable me in becoming a person, and to authenticate my personhood. To the extent that I am a person at all, and not merely a human individual, the achievement is not mine but his. No boot-strap procedure of theology or morality, or philosophy or science, could possibly do what he has done to and in me, and I can do no more and no less than celebrate his achievement.

"Why live?" In order to celebrate what God has done and is doing for me, for us all, for the whole creation from before the beginning of time. Because he cares enough about us to attack our ignorance, our hardness of heart, our comfortable despair. Because the quality of his attention toward us is not characterized by disinterested curiosity about what we may take into our heads to do next, or by the determination to train us willy-nilly as one breaks an unruly horse. Nor is it like the setting of a series of tests by which we can prove ourselves to him. He is not the amused observer of an entertainment, or the drillmaster coaching his squad, or the examiner bent on maintaining the highest standards for the degree. He cares what becomes of us for our sake, and is faithful to us even when we are faithless to ourselves and him. And for this quality and measure of concern we have only one word, inadequate and jaded though it is: he loves.

Why God should love is as inexplicable to me as why there should be a world, why we should be physical creatures and not pure minds, why human beings should be capable of becoming persons, why joy should be as meaningful as despair. At this stage of my theological journey, I neither know nor care very much why these things should be. What I do care about is that they are — or seem to be — facts: neither reasonable nor unreasonable, not susceptible to proof or disproof, and not dogmas of faith to be argued but conditions of existence to be accepted. My key to meaning, therefore, is not commitment but receptivity, not "I love" but "I am loved".

It had been love that starved me until I was eager to die, love that constrained me to fight for my life, love that nourished me, to the end that I would become able to accept love. I had been barred from knowing and welcoming love by my recalcitrant pride, especially in the forms of intellectual arrogance, moral self-righteousness, and imaginative sloth and cowardice. Always I had wanted to be loved; inexorably the Person of Love took me at my word. If I wanted love, I should have it, and since it is not possible to give or receive love on any terms except its own, the God of Love was prepared to destroy my resistance to love.

And he who gives himself into the hands of very Love will be saved from his enemies, as is promised, but nothing can save him from his Lover.

* * * * *

Like G. K. Chesterton and innumerable others, "I did try to found a heresy of my own; and when I had put the last touches to it, I discovered that it was orthodoxy." But I do not want to suggest that my theological journey has ended in the traditional faith. Christianity is a way of living, not a doctrinal conclusion. Even a Christian theology is not a finished product, but one phase in the continuing exploration of a story, told in the Gospels, that has infinite ramifications.

Because Christianity is grounded in a story, it can sustain many interpretations, from the childishly simple to the extremely elaborate, and to the simplicity of extreme wisdom. Each of us hears it differently against the background of his own life, and receives of it only as much as he can bear. Because it is a story, its form and content limit the range of its possible interpretations, yet allow for the growth of our receptivity and our capacity to endure its implications. And because it is a story, a tale, a narrative, and not an allegory or diagram or framework for a set of rules, the only way we can receive it is as we practise that most exacting of all the disciplines: by listening, by opening ourselves, by shedding our armor and becoming vulnerable to it. The emotions must be stilled or the noise of our demands upon life will deafen us. The intellect must be silenced or it will censor what we hear. We must put away our pride or we shall close our ears against every voice that is other than our own.

So far, I have emphasized the process by which I discovered how important it is to listen, and learned a few of the disciplines of listening. In what follows, the emphasis will be placed upon what I heard.

LIVING THEOLOGICALLY

It was the essence of Barbet's nature that he lived by no rules and yet had order within him, the order not of submission to laws or of conformity to the ideas of others but of his own sense of natural values. And yet, Courcelet said to himself, of what use is it to say that? A rebel, a man of anarchical mind, any vague and paltry upstart who wished to be conspicuous in his defiances, might claim to have "his own sense of natural values." The phrase is just a phrase — with truth in it if you know the man, but, if not, meaningless.

CHARLES MORGAN, *The Voyage*

chapter five

THE WAY OF INDIRECTION

Let no man be hasty to eat of the fruits of paradise before his time.

JEREMY TAYLOR, *The Life of Christ*

It is reasonable to suppose that once a basic theological position has been formulated out of the vigorous if rather messy interplay of action and reflection, the next steps — the tracing of its implications, its detailed application to behavior, its testing by experience, and its continual reformulation to reflect the outcome of those tests — will be comparatively clear-cut operations. Given the framework, all else will proceed by inference with the crystalline dexterity of philosophical and mathematical demonstrations.

This may be true for some theologians, both lay and professional. It has not been true for me. After labor and anguish I had discovered ground beneath my feet and had taken the stories of the Christian faith for my map in traversing that ground. But my adventures were not over. Some ancient maps show dangers — "Here there be Tygers" — and the charts I carried were of that kind. They could not tell me, however, at which bend in the road I was going to meet a Tyger, and although general directions were provided for coping with those and other beasts, I had to learn for (and usually by) myself what techniques to use with each individual one. Moreover, I met perils not listed in my guide books, not to mention well-marked roads requiring strengths or skills I did not have, and official as well as unofficial advisers whose counsel led me astray.

When the maps and the guides fail and unforeseen difficulties arise, what does one do? When one is lost, what methods shall he adopt to find himself? The next three chapters describe what

I did, and suggest how well or badly I have succeeded in finding my way and dealing with my particular Tygers.

The problems described in this chapter focussed my attention upon the present; those in Chapter 6 led me to come to terms with my past; and those in Chapter 7 directed me toward the future.

1. *The Experimental Life of the Spirit*

Out of my conviction that God is a person grew the increasingly firm conclusion that it was possible to have a continuing personal relationship with him. In addition, I deeply craved to enjoy consistently the sense of his immediate presence that had descended upon me intermittently. It took me between ten and fifteen years even to find a productive approach to the problem of how to go about establishing such a relationship, quite aside from developing one.

The intensity of my effort can be roughly measured by examining the kind and degree of my need. Those were the years when I was still hoping to bear or adopt children, and trying to reconcile myself to failure. During that time I came very close to intellectual and emotional ruin. Although my agony centered on my childlessness, other factors contributed largely to the turmoil. World War II and my brother's death in action. My husband's decision (in which I heartily concurred) to leave the pastoral ministry and go into college teaching. Our constant financial insecurity. Political and social changes, local, national, and international.

No doubt there are some who will censure me for not embarking forthwith on one or another program for political or social action, or teaching or studying or working in a church, or doing anything except undertaking an enterprise that looks all too much like a selfish and pompous effort to save my own little soul. Perhaps it was only that. Frequently I would have been glad enough to leave alone the religious and theological problems I was dealing with, but the problems would not cooperate by leaving me alone. Thus during my brief period of psychotherapy, the one question on which I completely blocked was, "Are you religious?" Being impressed as well as amused by the episode — which had many features in common with the earlier question, "Do you believe in fairies?" — I promptly delved into the religious phase of my existence, as contrasted with the theological.

That is, I started consciously to search for an adequate way to express, and thereby increase, my sense of the meaning in life, or in other words, to develop a devotional life that would supplement my burgeoning theology. Certainly I had praised and interceded and cried for help before this, but I had not before taken prayer as a central concern.

I began at the obvious place, with the teacher of my most valued teachers: Jesus called the Christ. My background of formal study of his message and life, and in the documents recording them, was extensive enough that I was better prepared for independent study than most laymen (though I am far from being a scholar). I was reasonably certain that Jesus could supply what I desperately sought, so it was with astonishment as well as dismay that I discovered my inability either to understand Jesus or to obey even the simplest of the Christian precepts. Indeed I could speak to him and have no doubt but that he knew what I was talking about. But I could not comprehend his responses. I could not even be sure that he was responding. For example, he commanded love. Over and over again I had read that the principle of love is so simple that a child can grasp it, and that failure to love indicated that one had failed in becoming as a little child. The fault was in me because I had not simplified myself. Therefore I tried to make myself simple and I tried to let him simplify me. Needless to say, both efforts were ineffectual.

Having found that I was too far from Jesus for his words to reach me, I turned to intermediaries: the great contemplatives and the masters of the devotional life. The instructions I obtained from a wide range of authorities can be condensed into a single imperative: establish a routine for praying, meditating, reading devotional literature, attending church, visiting the sick and the poor, and whatever other religious exercises were called for. Some authorities prescribed particular times of day or special postures or appropriate surroundings; some specified the proportion of time to be spent in this or that form of devotion. The variations appeared to be endless, but the prime requisite in every case was regularity. The success of the enterprise depended upon systematic practice.

It works. At least, everyone whose books or lectures I came across said that it does. Ministers preach that religious reading and prayer must be methodical. Religious directors assert that a firm order of procedure is indispensable for spiritual growth and stability. Theologians declare that regularity in worship is the fountain from which theological insights flow. These specialists know that it works. They are speaking out of long experience and profound study. To gainsay their observations and conclusions is to contravene a massive body of significant evidence on a well explored and rigorously tested way of life.

I repeat: it works. Then I must add: but it does not work for me. I simply cannot do it. I have tried over and over, changing all the elements and their arrangement. Sooner or later, invariably, my whole being revolts against the schedule as such in a manner sharply reminiscent of a healthy digestive system reacting against unwholesome food. Always my recalcitrant self has rebelled against every rule of life I have found, and I have censured myself bitterly for hardness of heart, sloth, negative attitudes, impatience, and culpable blindness, while I was in the very act of rejecting the counsels of the prophets and saints whom I longed to follow. I was racked with hunger for the bread of life to sustain my courage month by barren month, and to illuminate my mind in the round of piercing hopes, disappointments, frustrations, and monotonies. I took and ate gladly the bread that nourished others, and it sickened me.

My confusion and discouragement at this involuntary response was aggravated by the strong suspicion that it was satanic, a symptom of obstinate spiritual pride. Against that fear I have had no defense except the conjecture that a few persons may need a method of devotion entirely different from those prescribed by tradition. That surmise, however, has been consistently undermined by my failure to find even one authority on the subject who has suggested or implied that some other approach might be authentic, or possible, or at the very least suitable for those who are not ready to begin with the beginners. Surely if there were others who shared my disability, the classic writers on the life of the spirit would have spoken to — or at least of — their condition. Surely I could not be unique in my needs and capacities. Only a spiritual director could help me here, so I set myself to find one.

My ventures in that direction were such complete failures that I ended with the same dismal conclusion which terminated our hopes for conceiving or adopting children. If God wanted me to have one, he must provide it. Meanwhile, since I had to do something, I would stumble along on my own, charting a way for myself and trusting that God's mercy would forgive me and set me right if all I accomplished was the pampering of my proud and refractory heart.

I stopped importuning God to show himself to me. I prayed only when I felt like it, which was seldom. I did not read religious or devotional material unless it immediately caught my interest, which was rarely. When I went to church at all, it was for purposes other than worship and without expectation of worshipping. I abandoned all the universally recommended spiritual exercises, and substituted a discipline of relaxed, almost casual watching to see whether and when God would make his appearance, in the attempt to determine what would happen if instead of my cultivating God's presence, so to speak, I were to turn the initiative over to him.

Nothing happened except that bit by bit, with many intermissions and regressions, I began really to trust my own intuitions. Hitherto I had felt apologetic, if not guilty, when my inward responses had differed from what was prescribed. Consequently my spontaneity had been blocked and my judgment clouded until I was not sure what my honest responses were. Now I began to discover them, to listen to my own heart and think with my own head regardless of public or expert opinion. If I were damned or crazy or merely wrong, at least I would be so in my own way and not in others' ways.

The struggle first to find out what I did feel and think, and then to remain inwardly faithful to myself, has been long, silent, and for the most part solitary. During the middle of the process, however, I found one solid buttress to my courage, a passage by C. S. Lewis:

> For my own part I tend to find the doctrinal books often more helpful in devotion than the devotional books, and I rather suspect that the same experience may await many others. I believe that many who find that 'nothing happens' when they sit down, or kneel down, to a book of devotion, would find that the heart sings unbidden while they are working their way through a tough bit of theology with a pipe in their teeth and a pencil in their hand.

Since I could not worship when or in the way I was directed to, I would not try to worship, although neither would I refuse to pray or praise if I felt impelled to. I would neither seek nor resist but wait attentively and if possible patiently, theologizing only when — and if — I felt so moved.

My theologizing prepared me to recognize God when he came. It did not produce his presence. Nothing that I did was effective in bringing him to me or me to him. He seemed to come when and as he chose. But the overwhelmingly important fact is that he came. He did take the initiative. Always his coming was unexpected. If I prepared myself for his appearance, as at the great anniversaries of the Christian year, usually he absented himself. He has come on all sorts of occasions, so that I can never predict when I shall be invaded by that unmistakable presence or prepare for it, and he subjects himself to my initiative in only one circumstance: those moments when I cry for him to help me endure the onslaught of a joy too great to bear without his sharing it.

Generally he leaves me alone in my disasters, a phenomenon I would attribute to my own delinquency had he not shown himself perfectly capable of penetrating all my other frailties and barriers. In explaining the results of my experiments at such critical times, I must distinguish between two types of occasion: those in which there is something I can do, and those in which I can do nothing at all. The first type of occasion is common, and may be as complex as working out a major ethical problem or as simple as deciding whether to change the subject in a conversation with a friend. In these, I have learned by repeated, wretched experience that if I divide my attention by even a swift entreaty for divine guidance, I am lost. Nothing happens by way of answer, and I break the integrity of the event by injecting an alien element into it. When I take my eye from the work itself, even to pray, my hand slips.

Others can manage the blessed simultaneity of invoking God to their benefit in the midst of a job. I cannot with impunity even beg for assistance in restraining my fractious temper, or petition for insight into the problem I am facing. The exceptions to this general rule are rare, and are identifiable by the sign that in them I find myself spontaneously praying even though I do not want or intend to. While I am not entirely without religious resources in tense or confused situations, what helps me is not directly devotional. The discipline proper to me is to look at the situation in the light of my theology rather than to impose devotional attitudes and observances onto the occasion.

In the second type of situation, no action is possible except prayer, and in the critical instances that concern me here, I have been incapable even of mechanically repetitious prayer. I remember keeping vigil in a waiting room of a hospital where my mother was near physical death from disease and personal death from despair. For all one day and parts of several others, while God hid himself, my mind was irresistibly drawn to a theological problem I had never before considered: the virtue of hope — hope understood not as a feeling to be experienced but as a command to be obeyed. This was no detached speculation, but a fierce digging into the depths of human life in its direct relationships with nature and God. I was not praying; I was *thinking.* The thinking did not enable me to pray, but in one way it was the functional equivalent of prayer because by theologizing, I maintained a vital, if indirect, connection with the reality of God in spite of his withdrawal from my perception. Such a relationship is one of the chief ends of devotion, but in these situations I am more likely to achieve that end by the practice of theology than by any devotional practices.

Within very recent years, my devotional life has changed, but I am not yet ready to discuss either the process by which it happened or the forms that are beginning to stabilize. It may be that in time I shall be able to adopt the methods prescribed by the authorities on devotional and spiritual life. Or I may not. Meanwhile, the way which leaves the initiative to God is working for me, and the traditional ways are not working. I shall not try to hurry my progress or to force God's conclusions. Even admitting (as I willingly do) that the tradition is far wiser than I, I cherish Jeremy Taylor's admonition not to be hasty to eat of the fruits of paradise before my time.

I have not climbed to the level of the spiritual masters, and it is right for my practice to reflect my condition as a neophyte. Or perhaps I am climbing another face of the same mountain. Or perhaps I am altogether wrong. If so, I have every confidence that as long as I do not try to speed up the inherent rhythm of the process or to change its inherent direction, I shall be corrected and redirected when the time is ripe for it.

2. *The Fine Art of the Double Take*

The discovery that my devotional life was best sustained and nurtured indirectly, by theology, rather than by direct attention to spiritual disciplines, gave me the first hint of the possibility that indirection might be a general principle of all religious life — or of all my own religious life. The qualification is important because I have no idea how far this is applicable beyond myself. I have never heard or read a discussion of indirection as a religious principle, nor had opportunity to discuss it with theologians. So in this section, the reader should be even more wary of my conclusions than usual.

The everyday phenomenon of the double take illustrates one kind of indirection: the second perception that supersedes and transforms the first. A few minutes after nodding casually to a person on the street, it dawns on me that he looked familiar because I have seen his picture a hundred times in newspapers. Or long after a conversation is over, I suddenly grasp the import of a piece of information that had not registered at the time it was conveyed to me. Like the slow-witted character in the joke, I laugh in church on Sunday morning at the story I heard on Saturday night.

Most of my perceptions of God have been of this kind. Not until the event is completely over do I realize that it was he whom I had met in the situation. While it was occurring, I had rightly been caught up in what was going on. I was not thinking about God at all, but of the topic under discussion, the content and style of the book I was reading, the task under my hand, or the person talking with me. Not only is the double take my spontaneous manner of reaction; it seems also to be the only way I can function much of the time. At least, my attempts to circumvent its requirements are almost never successful.

Whatever may be the case for others, if I look for God in the sunset, I do not find him or anything else of value, although I may generate in myself an artificially pious emotional state that deludes me into thinking I have found something real or important or true. I do not deny that God reveals himself in sunsets, the wonders displayed by science, the Bible, and everywhere else. For myself, however, I discern him — if at all — after I have looked at the sunset for its own beauty, or studied the sciences for their own fascination, or read the Bible critically to find out exactly what it is saying and in what context it was said. When I treat almost any activity as a devotional tool, constraining it to serve my private objectives, it crumbles into meaninglessness.

The double take cannot be forced. The pun loses its humor

when it is laboriously analyzed. The core of the apple cannot be reached without breaking the skin. Learning the art of the double take has two phases: first, recognizing that it can be cultivated and disciplined into an invaluable technique, but that it has its own rules which are not the same as those for direct learning; and second, developing sensitivity in identifying the situations that carry the potentiality of a productive double take, yet restraining oneself from classifying them prematurely or forgetting them. It is the art of being tentative and patient and watchful, of immersing oneself in the present while action is going on, and reflecting upon the action when occasion permits.

The "single take" fails when I try to use it, for a reason which T. S. Eliot pinpoints in "East Coker": ". . . wait without hope/ For hope would be hope for the wrong thing." When I look for God in the sunset, for example, inevitably I am looking for the God I already know, my naturalized deity, my theological idol. But the God of worship and revelation is a God I do not already know. He has not yet disclosed himself to me, so I do not know where to look for him or what to look for. He is alien, astonishing in his strangeness. Or rather, I am the alien, and the more tenaciously I cling to the God of my own manufacture, who is the God I expect to see, the slower I shall be in finding the God who is not my creation but whose creature I am.

By now, I am fairly sure that God reveals himself most clearly — or I am most capable of receiving his self-disclosure — in the delayed reaction of the double take for the very reason that I am not looking for him then. The indirect vision, the allusion, the implicit suggestion, are his ways of eluding my natural tendency to create my gods in my own image. By a divine stratagem, he tricks me into dethroning my idols. I suspect that this may represent a characteristic pattern for others who may be on the way of indirection. Our discovery of God follows not from our directed attention, but from incidental perception which carries tremendous meaning because of the theological context in which the perception is secured. As the sight of a particular rock formation along the road, meaningless to me, may be highly revealing to a person with a rich background in geology, so an apparently trivial incident may be impressively significant to a person who is theologically minded.

From repeated experiences of such a kind, I have reached

the general conclusion that it is characteristic of God to function indirectly, and of nature to function directly. If we want to find the cause and cure of a blown-out fuse, or to construct an adequate theology, or to further social justice, we need to address ourselves directly to the problem. These are natural activities, although sometimes so complicated that in order to achieve the desired result, we have to start at the far edge of a problem or approach it slowly and from a considerable distance to one side.

Still, water applied to the roots of a wilting shrub will freshen its topmost leaves. Craftsmanship is acquired by instruction and steady practice. Houses are built and laws are passed by immediate application of means appropriate to those ends. Our sense experiences are the consequences of incredibly complex but direct chains of occurrence involving physical, physiological, and psychological elements in elaborate succession. Nature, as comprising all to which we give meaning, is the realm of direct action and direct knowledge, of the sciences, crafts, and theologies, of social organizations from local mores to international treaties, and of everything which can be taught and learned, investigated and observed, voluntarily undertaken and deliberately fostered.

In certain other areas, however, the methods of direct action and knowledge defeat their own purpose. No man becomes an original artist by striving for originality: the direct approach produces only an obviously derivative contrariety. The fashion for promoting "fellowship" as such is foredoomed because authentically personal relationships cannot be manipulated by direct techniques. Always they are the by-products of something else, often of shared work. The extreme example of indirection comes from God, who seems to have chosen to function for the most part indirectly through the physical universe, through human beings and histories and institutions, through intellects and prayers and the sciences and arts, and supremely in the act that is incomprehensibly direct and indirect at once, whereby he displayed in history his mediated Incarnation who was his unmediated self.

Direct action of some sort, however, is necessary for reaching the goals that in themselves are attainable only by indirection. To act indirectly does not mean to be passive, because something has to be done before anything can happen. The poet must master the grammar of his language before he can express whatever originality may be in him. A theology of some sort is a prerequisite to receiving a revelation, if only because without at least a rudimentary world view, no event can function revealingly. Carefully constructed social structures lay the indispensable foundation for personal encounter and communion. The temptation to by-pass the direct labor and to proceed forthwith to the rewards of indirection is constant and occasionally severe, but in yielding to it we commit the practical as well as theological error of failing to discriminate between appropriate and inappropriate means to a given end. God himself operates within and through nature, not apart from it. Our way, therefore, must also be natural and consonant with our own nature.

More critical than impatience is the common supposition that the results of the direct and the indirect ways are identical. A particularly good example comes from those people, sometimes deeply devoted Christians, who in the name of Jesus' injunction to become as little children, try by direct methods to create in themselves those qualities which are (or they believe to be) childlike. They are likely to declare that since the Gospel is simple enough for a child to understand, the huge mass of scholarship based on the records of his life is nothing but the expression of a perverse impulse to devise complications where none in fact exist. There is some justice in their point of view. Considering that a saintly theologian, at the end of a life devoted to scholarly research, may· voice his final judgment, "God is love," in the same words he learned as soon as he could utter the words, it would seem as if he had gained nothing from his minute analyses and erudite cogitations. The sage's indirectness and the child's directness have reached exactly the same conclusion.

But the simplicity of emptiness is not the same as the simplicity of integration. Those who reject intellectual inquiries into the faith they profess are thereby protecting their destitution, not their wealth. The child comprehends neither the richness and intricacy and greatness of life, nor the splendor and complexity and pertinence of the formula he parrots. He has the enchanting naïveté appropriate to his years and inexperience, which ought to be the prelude to sophistication. But to refuse sophistication is not a way of preserving childlike trust, any more than stunting physical growth is a way to prevent growing older. A simple-minded belief can have no relevance to the perplexities of adult experience, and the naïve who indulge their naïveté are soon enrolled in the appalling multitude of the gullible.

The mature have become like little children not by avoiding sophistication, but by going into and through and beyond it to a new simplicity which has the freshness of childhood without its crudity, a child's innocence without his frailty. The child-likeness of the Kingdom of God has the dynamic balance of a living human face, not the brittle stability of a painted portrait. It orders complexities instead of ignoring them, and turns invasions into occasions for illumination. Indeed the Gospels are simple enough for a child to hear and enjoy and learn from, but no child can plumb their depths or explore their heights, and no sophisticate can apprehend their integrity. To become mature in the Kingdom is to accept in turn both childhood and sophistication, and in turn to leave them behind when one outgrows them.

I have been writing of the direct and indirect ways, the single take and the double take, as if they were mutually exclusive. This has been deliberate, although I am well aware that it is misleading In any system whose elements are united by reciprocal action, the system breaks down if the differences between the elements be obscured. To give meaning to things — looking down at them, so to speak — is the reverse of looking up to receive one's meaning from others or an Other. To function directly is not the same as to function indirectly. Direct and indirect actions are different motions within the field, but they belong equally to the same total movement of maintaining and fulfilling relationships, and as every direct action has indirect consequences, so every indirect result presupposes a direct antecedent. They are interdependent and interpenetrating, diverse parts of a single integrated whole — a *uni*verse. Acting directly in nature, we receive indirectly the God whom we adore.

3. *The Adversary*

The God whom I do not know is my Adversary. We are locked in combat. That statement is not meant as a figure of speech or a paradox. I mean "combat" literally: I am fighting against his intention to make me what he wants me to be. I mean "locked": the battle has passed the stage when I could withdraw from it. I would have added "mortal" to "combat" if the combination were not so hackneyed, because my life is at stake.

I was brought up on the unqualified dictum that the primary duty of the Christian is to surrender to God in loving obedience, and that to resist him is useless as well as sinful. I agree. Only here, as in a number of other situations where I adhere with equal enthusiasm to traditional doctrines, I have learned that that ostensibly simple precept is like Einstein's formula $E=MC^2$, which summarizes and concludes a most intricate concatenation of observations and inferences. Thus to command a strongly self-willed person to submit quietly to God is as futile as to command a person overwhelmed by terror to relax. No matter how earnestly he resolves to obey, he cannot. Unless he is already relaxing or submitting to a fair degree, deliberate efforts to do so will only exacerbate his tension, so that the stress of trying to annul his natural reaction is added to what is already dominant.

When I set myself to surrender, I am assuming control over myself. Even though I were employing my will to enter the service of God, I would be exercising my freedom and initiative, and I would remain his servant by employing the volition which in theory I had relinquished. In fact, I would be obeying myself and not my Lord. Willed submission requires an act of the will, which raises the pivotal problem of how the will itself can be surrendered. How can we give up self-will except by willing? I do not know of any more penetrating comment on the problem of self-will than at the climax of J. R. R. Tolkien's *The Lord of the Rings,* where Frodo does not give up the ring; it is taken from him by force. At the very end of his quest, he cannot will to do what he must, and he succeeds only because he is overthrown.

The doctrine of Christian obedience declares that the human will must be destroyed so that it can be replaced by God's will. It is not enough for my will to choose its own master; I must be mastered. The all but universal inclination to be mastered has been interpreted as a regressive impulse toward infantile irresponsibility, but the regression may (and, I believe, often does) reflect an unconscious but accurate grasp of the radical human need to look up to something, as well as down at things and around to persons, and to yield to authority as well as to assert our authority. We are only half ourselves without an overarching sky, without something or someone to whom we are responsible and whose power over us gives meaning to the concept of responsibility. The delights and satisfactions of looking up were originally conveyed to most of us by our parents; they were infantile forms of joy. But the joy itself is not infantile, and we long for it because we are persons, not because we were children or are childish.

I am able to identify my authorities by their mastery of me. They resist me. They coerce me. They compel a response from me. I can hate them but I cannot refuse them. I can oppose them but I cannot deny them. Thus within the limits of my ability to reason logically, I cannot accept arguments that I see are illogical, and I manage to limit the authority of formal logic over my reason only by claiming that there are more varieties of logic than many philosophers are willing to concede: poetic logic, emotional logic, personal logic, and a number of others. My submission to the authority of reason — mind integrated with body and spirit — did not come automatically. I have learned both by precept and by the consequences of rebellion that reason is stronger than unreason, and stronger also than impersonal rationality. I have pitted my intellect against the authority of reason time after time, and always detachment has lost. In the same way, I have attacked nearly every new idea I have ever met. Unless I fight it, I cannot tell if it is stronger than I, if it is durable enough to trust. Unless it successfully resists me, I cannot depend upon it to support me.

It would seem that since I am intellectually persuaded of God's omnipotence, the process of testing him should be superfluous. Presumably it would be if I were completely at one with him already, knowing unmistakably who he is and what he wants of me. Unhappily, I do not know. Therefore I have found no way of identifying him as God except by ascertaining where an opposition to my wishes, intentions, and ideas has its source in him. I have already mentioned one critical battle of his will against mine, where mine finally broke. In my desperate, protracted efforts to bear or adopt children, my determination was intensified by the knowledge that failure would mean a fundamental redefinition of who I, as a person, was. It is not overstating the case to say that I saw myself as a natural or foster mother, or as nothing, and nothing was what I got.

I do not know of any way by which it can be proved that that breaking of my will was the act of God. It is indicative, no more, that my husband and I exhausted all the methods for overcoming infertility then known, as well as the legitimate adoption agencies operating in the areas where we successively lived. Since our defeat could not be ascribed to our inaction or stupidity, it was reasonable to consider ascribing it to the divine will. A second indication is suggested by the ultimate discovery of the inherent biological defect in me which permanently closed one of the doors to my desire. A third is suggested by what followed my admission of defeat. After I abandoned my own intentions — which is to say, my definition of my own meaning — I was too exhausted and too unsure of myself to choose or hunt for another definition. Almost in so many words, I informed the good Lord that the next move was up to him. The challenge had nothing in it of noble renunciation or exalted acquiescence. It held no trace of the creative reconciliation implied in, "not my will, but thine, be done." It was instead the nasty, childish retort, "Okay, you do it." And he did. He opened to me a vocation which I am sure is his will for me because I was pushed into it, and because it has led me where I never expected, intended, or (sometimes) wanted to go.

Certainly I embarked willingly upon my work as a writer, and have loved it. And I was not completely passive, by any means, in starting or continuing the work. It was by choice that I wrote an interpretation of Charles Williams' novels in an attempt to share my solitary enthusiasm for them. It was by choice that I sent it forth when it was finished, and accepted the suggestion of Mr. Raymond C. Goffin of the Oxford University Press that I expand the material into a book. God put me in a situation where writing was one of the obvious possibilities, and I was alert to respond. However, writing was not my first or only choice. Before settling down with pencil and typewriter, I had tried a number of other activities, all temporarily or partially satisfying, but either their insufficiency became apparent or circumstances (God?) prevented my continuing with them.

From those experiences and other similar ones, I have concluded that my own judgment on my nature and place in the world is not to be trusted. God has created me for certain purposes and not for others, to become one kind of person and not another. He has not seen fit to bestow upon me any direct enlightenment regarding his intentions, so I had better be chary of trying to anticipate him, lest I spend another ten years in another fruitless attempt to make myself what I want to become. I am better off accepting what life gives me than in making demands upon life, better off acquiescing in my spontaneous preferences and impulses than in trying to predetermine my responses so that they will fit into a pattern of my choosing. Thus although I admire serenity more than any other personal quality except courage, I have long since accepted the fact that temperamentally I am impetuous, cyclic, intense, and in the worst sense enthusiastic. I need very badly — and work very hard — to channel my violent impulses toward good ends. So far, self-mastery has a legitimate function. What would not be legitimate would be the deliberate effort to make myself serene.

There are three possibilities here; I have rejected the first two of them. First, I could compress myself into the mold of serenity. Second, I could reject all self-direction and become subject to every momentary whim. Third, I could place under discipline my actions but not my self. If I take proper care of what I do, I can expect that what I become will take care of itself. Conceivably my attempts to do good may sometime flower into my being good, although I suspect that even in heaven I would not display a tranquil style of goodness. But when I act in terms of the situations God places me in, recognizing his function in them, I discover indirectly his purpose for me, and he creates indirectly the person he wants me to be, and so the transformation is effected not by my will but by his.

It would seem as if my deliberate intention to obey God ought to nullify the statement that God is my adversary. It is reasonable to suppose that God wants his creatures to do what is good and to inform themselves about what is good. So far as they succeed, is he not their ally rather than their adversary? Such a formulation of the problem in terms of ethics is hallowed by civilized tradition but not by traditional Christian theology. The ethical life, like the theological life and the devotional life, is man-made, whereas sanctity is the work of God, and the goal of Christianity is sanctification and not righteousness. The saints are by definition righteous, but the righteous man is not necessarily a saint, and he who concentrates upon making himself righteous is in danger of hindering sanctification by the intensity of his efforts, which can very well inhibit his receptiveness to the supreme quality of life that transcends righteousness.

Ethics, theology, and worship are essential for Christianity, as technical exercises are essential for the musician and grammar for the writer. The need for them is never outgrown or annulled, but they should not be permitted to become ends in themselves. They must be taken up into a greater activity and made instruments for purposes far beyond themselves. As a writer, I am profoundly grateful for having been taught to diagram a sentence and to outline an essay. As a Christian, I am equally grateful for my ethical and theological training. But I do not want to be a grammarian or a moralist or even a theologian. I want to be a writer and a saint: to become an adequate agent for the transmission of a quality of existence that I do not possess and shall never possess by my own efforts, but only by the incredible magnanimity of God.

Sanctification is something that God does. I can do nothing toward that end, nor should I try to. But on the principle that unless something is done, nothing can happen, I must act. So I return to the demand for righteousness but in a new setting that changes its meaning. I am no longer called to perfect my will. The stress is no longer on "What should I do?" but rather on "What needs to be done?" as the center of concern shifts from the self to the situation. Similarly, I must act with respect to my preferences, because in preferring I most clearly function integrally. I can educate my preferences by directly training myself in ethical, intellectual, aesthetic, and other discriminations. And I must express my preferences by incarnating them in action; which is to say, by expressing myself; which is to say, by exposing myself to destruction, and by being destroyed.

Since destruction can come from a myriad of sources — social and economic pressures, physical and mental compulsions, the impact of evil on good and of better upon best — I must find a way to differentiate God's destructiveness from others', and so to determine which of my adversaries is the Adversary. The only answer I have yet found is that he alone consistently builds where he has destroyed. He alone raises from the dead that which he has allowed to be overthrown.

I war against God to make certain that it is he who is opposing me, and it is a joyous battle. I can fight him with every atom of my strength because I am utterly confident in him. He is tough: my attacks will not hurt him, my reproaches will not annoy him, my rebellion will not deter him. Any damage which ensues is done to me. Further, by resisting him I become vulnerable to him. Becoming vulnerable, I am afraid of what he may do to me next. Admittedly, I am fearful of dying even in part, and I know myself to be as fearful of his life as of my death. Deliberately, therefore, I oppose him in order to keep vulnerable and to be broken, so that finally he may raise me from the dead.

I describe my war against God as a matter of record, not as a suggestion or recommendation to anyone else. I am not at all sure that I approve of it, and I can justify (rationalize? excuse?) the enterprise only by the frail argument that this is what I have found myself doing. When I first identified what was going on, I was so horrified that I immediately tried to stop it. I apologized, so to speak, and withdrew. The withdrawal, however, did not forestall further combat. After repeated withdrawals and renewals of the battle, I decided to see what would happen if, instead of vainly trying not to fight God, I were to deliberately fight him, like Jacob with the angel and Job with Yahweh. Thus far, it seems to have worked.

The future must see to itself, but as of now, every episode in our battle has strengthened my trust in his power, and also in his love, his efficiency, and his responsiveness. Although I am still afraid of what he may have in store for me, and not infrequently resentful of what he is doing to me, and continually tempted to retire from the battle to a place of safety, I know all too well that to be safe from God is to die the death from which no one is raised, to turn from being a person into a thing, and from a thing into an unreality.

4. *The Breaking of the Silence*

The battles and experiments reported here have been conducted under a shroud of reticence so complete as to constitute secrecy. I have discussed with several people, notably my husband, some of the general theological concepts, relationships, and problems that are involved, but seldom the religious impulses behind them, and never the material in this chapter. The reasons for concealment are defensible; its desirability is questionable.

Behind all the other reasons for silence has stood one simple obstacle. Until recently I have had no language in common with others for expressing to them what was happening in and to me. Without at least a private language, we cannot think at all. Without a shared language, we cannot communicate anything except our emotional disturbances, to the bewilderment of our companions and our own shame. We try to get help and are thwarted because we do not know what kind of help to ask for, and they do not know what kind of help to give. Conversely, we try to help them, but have nothing to say except "It's all right" in situations where, if anything at all is right, it is exceedingly well hidden. Some such difficulties can be resolved by more careful definitions. Others raise harder problems, because their solution depends upon basic conceptions and definitions with which neither we nor our associates may be familiar.

A language is not merely a collection of verbal symbols. Far more important, it is a structure of thought, a conceptual framework embodied in a grammar and exhibited by the ways in which the words are used. Moreover, most languages can be used in more than one way. For example, the proposition, "All men are mortal," can be uttered and heard as a logically transparent statement or as a cry of existential anguish, and it can be spoken in one way and interpreted in the other. Unless its context is understood as logical or existential, one cannot determine which of these two widely divergent but wholly legitimate meanings it carries.

Existential questions can no more be dealt with by strictly logical argument than historical problems can be answered by the physical sciences, but until I had learned to differentiate between logical and existential propositions, I could neither speak clearly nor be understood. Thus, however nebulous and chaotic the foregoing (and forthcoming) narrative may be, it is a marvel of lucidity compared with what went on in my mind while I was experiencing the events here described, before I had a language for understanding them and stating them to others.

Ideas are only the tools of thought, and words only the carriers of ideas, but we cannot think without them. This first barrier to communication, however, is not essentially verbal because once we arrive at the ideas, we are likely to have a host of words to express them with. It is primarily conceptual, stemming from an insufficiency in categories, distinctions, and all the other instruments for exploring what is already in our experience, and for enlarging it.

The second barrier to communication followed directly from the first by the importunate logic of emotion. My inability to communicate, or to find anyone who could communicate with me, led me to believe that "spiritual" things ought not to be spoken of at all. It seemed obvious that if they were acceptable topics for social conversation or intellectual discussion, I would long since have been taught a language for them, or would find one readily available when I needed it. Since no such language seemed to exist, my desire to talk about religious and theological matters must be improper if not indecent. As a corollary, even to undergo such experiences as my dream and my questioning must be proof positive that something was seriously wrong with me. It was good to keep silent about those events, better to forget them, and best not to have gone through them at all.

The distress produced by the silence, as it resulted from inadequate language and from shame, was compounded by the frustration resulting from attempts to talk about the meaning of life with persons who were simply not interested in the subject, or were afraid to examine it, or had prematurely crystallized their ideas about it. One cannot infallibly determine in advance who will rebuff him with the bludgeon of indifference or the bright sword of hostility, and it does not take much discouragement of that kind to stifle curiosity and stunt growth. My tentative approaches were dismissed with the epithet "morbid", or the conversation was ostentatiously deflected to entirely different subjects, or the discussion was transferred from the existential to the logical level, which was quite enough to persuade me, before long, that the better part of wisdom is secrecy.

One more reason for silence needs to be mentioned. It does not require much imagination to realize that some consequences of withdrawing the current taboos upon existential discussion of the religious life will be evil. One need only observe what has happened since conversation about sex was granted social approbation to see that although great good has undoubtedly followed, the consequent evil has also been great, ranging from tasteless inanities at the dinner table to massive philosophical systems predicating that man is made in the image of the phallus. Sex has been publicly denatured, depersonalized, cheapened, denigrated, and idolized. A normal and indigenous act has been treated as if it were the most esoteric of the arts, to be approached only after ritual preparation by courses of lectures or reading, and in the preposterous belief that sexual adequacy is conclusive evidence of intrinsic personal fulfilment.

If we begin opening our religious lives to one another, cautious though we be to discriminate regarding circumstances, persons, and manner of presentation, similar corruptions will inevitably follow, in worse degree because the material of religion is more complex, more subtle, and more intimate even than sex, and more is at stake. To expose such ideas in the market place lays them open to ridicule, vulgarization, disdain, and shameless misrepresentation, in addition to entirely valid and immensely valuable honest, intelligent disagreements. In breaking silence, we give our most intimate selves to the power of the dogs.

Yet we have the duty to break our silence and to leave the safety of our seclusion, to the extent that we can and as opportunity permits. It is not good to fabricate occasions or to trample down our spontaneous aversions to speech, but neither is it good to recoil from another's need or to allow ourselves to be victimized by timidity. If the inward life is unshared, or if it issues forth only in acts whose source is deliberately concealed, it ultimately festers or becomes sterile. The word that has been spoken to us must, in turn, be spoken by us or it will perish in the darkness where we have hidden it.

The damage done by unnecessary and unseemly reticence is widespread, including both public and private injury. This book should be sufficient witness to the crippling effects of working in solitude. In recent years, I have come across a number of other persons who bear similar scars and equivalent disabilities, many of which are likewise traceable to their failures in locating anyone with whom to share either the word they have received or the problems they were confronting. It may be argued that loneliness weeds out all but the tough-minded and the thick-skinned, and smothers the erratic and the feeble, as if the spiritual life ought to exhibit the survival only of the fittest. But authentic perception is not invariably conjoined with exceptional fortitude or obstinacy, and the world is not yet so radiantly illuminated that it can do without the smaller lights which will die if their flames are persistently checked.

The search for a language is a search not only for clarification, but also for community. My method of searching was clumsy and unpromising, and as usual, I did not really know what I was searching for until I had found it. What I did was to scout around haphazardly to see what might speak to my condition. Then after trying it out and following any leads it offered, I would discard whatever did not ring true to me and continue working along any lines that appeared hopeful. During these ten or fifteen years, only two persons consistently approached the level of my need, and even they fell short: C. S. Lewis and Dorothy L. Sayers. Almost none of their work conveyed the flavor which my dream had had; therefore they could not teach me a language adequate for integrating the dream with my theology and my world. But they baptized my mind and taught me how to use the compass of reason in the realm of religion. They set my face toward Jerusalem and companioned me as I began my journey. My debt to them is immeasurable. And through them, although not from them, I found both the language and the community I sought.

In November of 1949, a friend called my attention to an article by Geoffrey Parsons in the current *Atlantic Monthly,* about an English author named Charles Williams who had known and influenced Mr. Lewis and Miss Sayers, as well as other writers whose work I admired. With no more and no less anticipation than had sustained my other explorations, I read the article and applied to the college library for any of Williams' books that might be obtainable by Interlibrary Loan from the nearest university. They came: *All Hallows' Eve* and *Descent into Hell.* And I recall being somewhat annoyed at having to pay a dollar and a half for borrowing the two novels. As I remember, it was a Monday morning when I started reading *All Hallows' Eve;* by night I had finished it. The next day I read it again. The following day I turned with trepidation to *Descent into Hell,* half expecting that it would disappoint me. If anything, it was better.

In one stroke, those two novels gave me a new world, a new language, and a new community. They initiated me into a new life that included my old one, but transformed it by giving both my present and my past a new meaning. In this astonishing new world, I was at home as I had never before been at home in any place or time or with any people. The accents of its language were familiar to me at first hearing. I recognized instantly the main outlines of its geography and customs. Here I was both secure and free, possessing at once integrity of my own and integration with others. With an almost tangible movement, proportions shifted, needs and demands slid into fresh patterns, some problems dissolved and others crystallized. Life suddenly became infinitely richer, more complex, subtler, safer, more dangerous, and more exhilarating than I had ever dreamed of its being, and now that I had found it, I knew for the first time what it was that I had been striving for all my life: not to know something, but to be known.

The world and community into which Charles Williams inducted me were not his creation. He was merely one of their most recent expositors. Their nature will be sketched as the discussion proceeds; here I want to say only that they are profoundly Christian, although his presentation is not couched in traditional terms. It is based on the concept of the co-inherence, the ordered exchange of functions which, having its source in God, is no more restricted by time and space than he is.

Inevitably, my introduction into this new world created difficulties, of which the first and most pressing was the need to relate my old world with the new one in such a way that I could communicate fully with those around me who were not acquainted with the new. I soon discovered that I could do so only by learning to translate between the two languages, specifically by explaining the relationship between Williams' method of imagery and the method of allegory which most of the people I knew used in their thinking. Out of that effort to translate came my book on Williams' theology.

Meanwhile, however, I was confronting problems of personal adjustment and development that could not wait upon a full solution of the language problem.

5. *The Community of Exchange*

The process by which a person is made new by his entrance into a new world can best be presented by starting with a simple illustration. When I was nine or ten years old, a school nurse discovered that I was badly near-sighted. I remember nothing of the announcement to my parents, the examination by an oculist, or any effect my glasses had on my school work. All that remains to me now is the extraordinarily vivid memory of standing in Potwin School yard, feeling my glasses tickle my nose, and seeing with incredulous awe that the great trees along the east edge of the playground had separate leaves all the way up.

Even as a child I realized that this was a significant event, although I had only a glimmering of where its significance lay or how much was contained in it. Then I knew only that I was certainly going to be taunted by my playmates with the epithet "Four-eyes" — glasses for children were not common in those days — and hungry though I was for acceptance by my peers, I cared not one single, solitary whit. They could call me anything they pleased. I had a brand new marvel of a world to live in, to investigate, and to adore.

I had lived in one world, and now I lived in another. What the old world was like is reproduced in miniature when circumstances require me to go without my glasses for a period of some hours, and the easiest way to describe the difference is by saying that at such times it takes conscious effort to keep from huddling in a corner where at least I have something solidly definable behind me. I cannot tell if an approaching figure is stranger or friend, or accurately identify a movement, until it has come so close that I have almost no time to prepare myself for responding appropriately. I strongly suspect that if I had been without glasses for a few years longer, I would have become pathologically schizophrenic.

In place of a world where everything beyond arm's length was blurred and uncertain, I now had a world where I could define entities and anticipate events. The extension of my horizon, of the area within which I could see clearly, deepened my confidence in the world as well as in myself. I could move more firmly among distinct things and persons than among the obscurities I had previously known.

The impact of that change precluded regret that my disability had not been diagnosed earlier. Had I been much younger, the moment of change would have been less poignant and therefore less meaningful. Further, in the long run it precluded regret that I am near-sighted. Had I not been, the core of the affair might have escaped me. I have already described one aspect of that core: I had lived in one world, and now I lived in another. The second and more important is this: as a result, I became another person. I did not first achieve a fresh psychological orientation and then see the world in a new light. Rather, I first saw a new world and then, in response to it, I became new. In technical terms, the alteration in my metaphysic decisively altered me psychologically.

Exactly the same thing happened when, through Charles Williams, I saw the world of the co-inherence. The fact that one change of worlds was inaugurated by a physical perception and the other by an intellectual impression may be interesting, but is irrelevant to the structure of the events. In both cases, my world turned around in front of me, and the change in its character, as I knew it, initiated the change in me. Thus prior to my meeting with Charles Williams' description of the world, I had taken for granted that the fundamental laws of human association required me to stand on my own feet as much as I possibly could, lest I become a burden to others — and they had enough troubles of their own without taking care of mine. As a Christian, I believed myself duty bound to observe the injunction about the superior virtue of giving over receiving which the author of the book of Acts quotes Paul as having attributed to Jesus.

In my new world, I recognized that my attempts to stand on my own feet were not only impossible, but also offenses against the web of interactions by which my whole life was and had always been sustained. My resolute independence was both an illusion and a sin, and unless I learned to receive gladly and gratefully the gifts I had hitherto spurned or accepted as my rights, I would never be able to give freely or in love. Until I consented to being borne, I could not help to bear the burdens of others. The supreme blessedness lay not in giving but in the exchange of gifts. It might still be more blessed to give than to receive, but receiving was the precondition for giving — our very lives are a gift to us — and it is best to share beatitude by participating joyously in the reciprocity of the community of exchange.

I do not find it easy to receive. My tenacious pride rebels when I cannot repay a gift instantly to my benefactor, preferably in the same coinage. But it is intrinsic to the way of exchange that often the movement should be passed on instead of back, thereby bringing others into consciousness of the network and extending the life of deliberate exchange. So exact is the equilibrium of the process that what I do not repay, another will, and what is not directly repaid to me will be repaid indirectly. My primary function is to receive freely and give freely, leaving it to the efficiency of the Omnipotent to balance the books.

This one point of comparison between the two worlds will

serve for the moment to indicate what changes in attitudes and manner of living were involved in my transfer from one to the other. Perhaps it should be added that although the metaphysical break was relatively abrupt and clean cut, the resulting alterations in myself were gradual and not outwardly conspicuous. My temper did not promptly become seraphic. I was not immediately released from my recurrent attacks of psychological anxiety and spiritual despair. I continued to indulge myself in detective stories and to neglect dusting baseboards and waxing floors. I did not take myself to long or systematic prayers or become assiduous in attending church. All in all, I behaved just about as before. The essential change lay far deeper than overt behavior or the conscious mind, and worked its way to expression in daily life over a period of many years.

In the long run, the most decisive changes in me resulted not from knowing the new world — knowing is a relatively minor accomplishment — but in apprehending that I was known. To understand the full significance of this discovery, it must be recalled that personal development is a product of personal communication, and that communication is a form of exchange, of giving and receiving. The poles of personal exchange are knowing and being known, and here indeed is the definitive distinction between personal and impersonal relationships, since we know a thing without its knowing us, but we cannot know a person except as we permit ourselves to be known. When the psychologist and the sociologist and we ourselves know other human beings without being known by them, we are relegating ourselves — together with them — to the category of things. As I have indicated earlier, such impersonality is sometimes necessary. All of us must at times be impersonal even with ourselves, or else practically none of the world's work would get done. But to the degree that we are not known, our natures as persons remain undeveloped.

When I was a child, I had longed for someone who would understand me perfectly — what child does not have that dream? As I grew older, I began to comprehend that perfect understanding by any other person, even if it were possible, would be intolerable, so ugly were some recesses of myself, so fragile the beauty of others. At one time I defined hell as complete awareness of what one has done; on such a basis, the nadir of hell would be to have someone else know exactly who and what one is, to be utterly exposed with no shred of veiling. I still think that this would be a worse doom than any pictured in Dante's *Inferno,* and that perfect illumination by the full radiance of the divine light is the most terrible sentence that could be passed upon anyone. By the mercy of God, however, my discovery that I was indeed known was accompanied by the discovery that I was forgiven. The community of exchange was a community of the forgiven and therefore of the forgiving.

I did not deserve forgiveness — but then, no one deserves to be forgiven. There is nothing anyone can do to deserve it. It is not a reward for merit, or a compensation for repentance, or a right to which we are entitled by desire or Christian baptism. In my own case, heretofore I had had no special sense of needing more forgiveness than presumably was already mine by virtue of my reasonably clear-sighted recognition of my shortcomings and my reasonably consistent efforts to improve myself. In brief, I had not known what forgiveness is. Until the burden of sin had been lifted from my shoulders, I did not realize how it had encumbered me.

Because my sin and my sins were forgiven, I could bear their being known. Because they were not overlooked or contemptuously belittled, my personal responsibility was confirmed, and my identity as a person was established — not by myself, but by those who knew me and through whom I now began to know myself. Self-knowledge was the product of an indirect, not a direct, view: of seeing how others responded to me instead of gazing into the mirror of introspection. Charles Williams gave me a world whose citizens and Lord responded to me in a new way, the way of exchanged forgiveness, and I became a new person in response to their new knowledge of me.

It seems strange to speak of being known by other persons when at that time, I was aware of only one human being who knew me in the way of exchange: Charles Williams himself, who had died five years before I had even heard of his existence. The key to that anomaly lies in the nature of knowledge itself, which is the product of interactions between the knower on the one hand, and on the other of the known things and persons around him. In his books, Williams spoke to me personally. That is, he spoke in a way that stirred not merely my intellect and emotions, but also that precise though undefined personal center which functions intellectually and emotionally, as well as volitionally and physically. Because he spoke from that center in himself, and I responded from my equivalent center, a personal relationship was created even though we were not and could not be directly acquainted. Williams could not have written as he did unless he had known persons sufficiently like myself that their experience flooded mine with light. The fact that the books were written demonstrated that I had companions. The fact that they had been published and were being read demonstrated the existence of still others. And because Williams, his other readers, and myself co-inhered in God and followed the way of exchange by the power of God, we were effectively united without regard to the temporal and spatial discontinuities that separated us.

In one sense I had no conclusive evidence for the existence of the community of exchange except as it consisted of Williams and myself, and I was not entirely sure that I was interpreting him correctly. Only one or two of my immediate associates appeared to grasp what he was talking about, and they did not appear to take it with any great seriousness. In another sense, the evidence was amply conclusive because the diagram of the glory which Williams displayed not only rang true to me as an individual person; it also rang true to me as a member of the community which he described sometimes in fictional, sometimes in non-fictional form.

So, after all these years, my private criterion of truth was transmuted into a public one. In the community of the co-inherence, the opposition between free development of individuality and full communion in a society was healed, because here the intensification of uniqueness and the deepening of common life were interdependent. An action that disrupted the community of exchange also weakened the personal identity of its members. An offense against the individuality of one concurrently loosened the bonds of union. "What rings true to me" was here indistinguishable from "What rings true to us". The astonishing identity of the "us" with the "me" seems to be possible only among those who willingly exchange their lives and functions with one another, gladly receiving and gladly giving, because only here is the polarity upon which full communication depends to be found fully developed. Within that community we sometimes disagree or even conflict, but sharing the same criteria of truth and goodness — the furthering of exchange

— and sharing the same life, we have immediately at hand a method of reconciliation within our disagreements.

We do not and cannot know what the world is in itself. We can only decide what kind of a world we will live in. I have chosen to live in the kind of world that Williams delineates, and to my delight, in recent years I have become directly acquainted with an increasing number of others who have made the same choice. Many of them have never heard of Charles Williams. Some know almost nothing about Christianity. Most of us have reached our conclusion independently, and have held to it faithfully during long periods when we were isolated from others who consciously lived by the acts of exchange, the co-inherence, under any name or in any form. We are not formally organized into an institution or society or religious order, but neither is our relationship unformed. It is indeed highly structured, but its structure is derived from the interplay of diverse functions which constitutes the way of exchange, and is therefore infinitely flexible. It is perceptible everywhere, but definable only in terms of the concrete, historical events where human exchanges incarnate the divine Person from whom the principle of exchange is derived.

chapter six

THE SINS OF THE FATHERS

She had been lost in a high marvel, but if that joy were seriously to live it must somehow be reconciled with the agony that had been . . . "How can we be happy, unless we forget? and how can we forget? how can we dare forget?"

He said: "Forget nothing. Unless everything's justifiable, nothing is. . . ."

CHARLES WILLIAMS, *Descent into Hell*

Setting forth on the way of exchange, I realized almost at once that I was stringently limited in fulfilling the new life by habits, attitudes, and loyalties formed in the past and so firmly embedded in my present self that I could not free myself from them. I was bound to a history that obstructed every present motion toward the co-inherent life, and if I were to make any headway at all, I would have to come to terms with my past. In particular, I was hampered by sheer ignorance of what can be done about the past and how to do it, and then by my heritage of legalism, individualism, egocentricity, and sin.

1. *The Unanswerable Question*

My earliest memory is of standing in a grove of pine trees, crying my two-year-old heart out in an abandonment of rage and frustration because I could not get an answer to a perfectly reasonable question. Nearby there was a house built on the side of a hill, and I merely wanted to know whether the floors in the house were parallel with the slope of the ground, or horizontal. The first alternative was clearly not practicable, but since it did not occur to me that a chunk of Colorado mountain could

126

be cut away to make space for a building, the second did not seem practicable either. It was not the thwarting of my curiosity, however, that so deeply disturbed me, but my utter defeat by a failure in communication. I could not make anyone understand what my question was; therefore it was not only unanswered, but unanswerable.

I know of nothing, my whole life through, that has so consistently baffled and infuriated me as an unanswerable question, whether because it is not understood, or because it is understood and despised, or because it is used as an opportunity to bait the questioner. My flaming fights with my father almost always revolved around the meaning and legitimacy of my questions. He, being preoccupied with his own problems in constitutional law, was prone to dismiss mine as trivial. I, of course, retaliated with increasingly frantic insistence upon their importance.

The topic I remember most clearly — I am sure that it came up many times — had to do with the discrepancy that sometimes arises between law and equity. Often at the dinner table, my father would describe a case which was being presented before the federal court of which he was a judge, outline the relevant laws and statutes, and then ask the three of us children to state and defend our verdicts upon it. This was not an entertainment at which I excelled, since invariably I was concerned with what seemed to me just, and cared next to nothing about legal precedents and minutiae of phrasing. I felt dimly, naggingly, that while the terms of social organization seemed to preclude equity in some affairs, yet there must be a way in which it could be fulfilled without destroying society. My father's general position — that since men are imperfect, justice must also be imperfect, and for the sake of society the individual must accept inequity with the same grace that he would accept losing an athletic contest or a bridge game — was not only unsatisfying to my intellect; it was also obscurely an affront to my sense of the integrity of the world.

My father died long before I was able to phrase my questions about equity and justice in a way that he could see what I was struggling for. In any case, I am not sure that he could have answered those questions, because he was operating within one context and I was operating within a different one, defined both by my immaturity and by my level of concern. He was engaged in determining and defining the principles which would provide, on the whole, the highest degree of justice that is compatible with a society established on the Constitution of the United States. For me, that was not enough. I wanted — I do not know what I wanted, except that it was something more adequate to the intricacies of individual human beings, and more perceptive of the intrinsic nature of man and society.

I now see those frequent disputes as exemplifying the entire problem of the relationship between personal beings and impersonal entities such as laws and institutions, and believe its solution possible in terms of the co-inherence and the life of exchange, but that is beside the point. The immediate issue is the implicit denial that my questions about the relation of law to equity were proper ones. In effect, it seemed to me that the treatment of my questions as unimportant or foolish reflected the judgment that I as a person was unimportant if not ridiculous. If, as a person, I were important to my father, he would have taken the trouble to find what my level of discourse was, and to explore the questions with me until together we could define and answer them, and so heal my wound. Although now I am sure that this was a tragically false conclusion — I have no doubt of his love for me or mine for him — still, that was the way I felt when we were arguing.

I have not dredged these unhappy incidents out of their graves in order to show how certain of my present attitudes developed, even though they may go a long way in explaining the psychological tensions which pushed me into theology. The display of the past may generate pity or persuade the sentimental to condone my sins, but it is my present self with whom I — and others — have to deal: the present self who is still enraged to the point of helpless incoherence when the legitimacy of a serious question is denied. But the clear understanding of the past does not help me to handle myself now, any more than archaeology can solve contemporary political problems.

Such legacies from my childhood and adolescence remain possessions that I cannot get rid of. I cannot forget them, and if I could, I would still be unable to escape their permanently injurious effects. To dig into the question of why they should have happened would lead only to an infinite regress of answers, especially since a determinative factor in the situation was the ordinary, straightforward collision of closely similar temperaments, with each person fearing and hating in the other those traits he most feared and hated in himself.

The natural response to an unfortunate heritage is resentment directed toward the necessity that resulted in harm, if not toward the person who occasioned the harm. The common sense response is to shrug it off: "All right, so it happened and it was bad. Holding a grudge is a waste of time and energy. Write it off. Let it go." The psychiatrist's response depends upon the particular school of thought he belongs to, but it frequently involves teaching the patient to express in socially acceptable ways the frustration, the bitterness, the primitive terror of being rejected, that have been dammed up since the events occurred, thus leading him into freedom from them. The Christian response is still different: to become free by means of and within them.

Christianity begins by accepting — or defining — as fact that the sins of the past, both my father's and my own, have been visited upon me. While my father was alive, we were together in sin; now that he is dead, those sins live on in me and because they persist, they are accessible to my present actions. To the degree that their consequences are used for good, the sins are converted from evil into good, and to the degree that I am willing to act toward that end, I not only release myself from the burden of our common sin, but in some sense my father is also released from it. Probably we could have done a better job of redemption together, but because he did not live to do it, the responsibility rests upon me.

The sins of the fathers are laid upon us, their children, not as punishments but in order that we may participate redemptively in the lives of our forebears. They gave us our physical and personal lives; by the grace of God, we can give of ourselves in return, by doing for them what they could not do for themselves. My father could not turn his irritation at me into good for either of us, but I can turn it into good — or rather, since the conversion of evil into good is possible only to God, I can help by consenting to share in the process which God initiates and sustains. Or I can refuse any part in it by clutching my resentment to my breast and refusing to change. I can transmit the sin or join in transmuting it. Because God is omnipotent, the sin has been or can be redeemed; the question for me is whether or not I shall participate in its redemption.

We are not free to chose what heritage we shall receive from the past or, for that matter, what will happen to us today or tomorrow or any time. We are free, however, to choose how we will respond to what happened and happens, destructively or redemptively. We are free to pass on our heritage of evil to our children and neighbors and colleagues, or to use it for good and so transform it into good. So one result of the agony I went through with my unanswerable questions about law and equity was that I developed a passion for personal as opposed to formal relationships. I did not plan in advance to use the experience in such a way. My father certainly did not intend for me to learn such a lesson when he battered my fragile defenses. The redemption here was unintentional on my part, but it was none the less an authentically redemptive activity because to that degree the evil brought forth good. And to the degree that other aspects of our antagonism can be used for good, it will be more fully redeemed.

The redemption of evil is not automatic even when it is unintentional, and it is not easy. It is a costly purchase. This we are likely to take for granted in such natural redemptions as the healing of physical disease, and we are prepared to pay heavily for diagnosis and treatment both in money and in cooperation. When it comes to personal and social evils, however, we appear to expect healing by fiat or miracle. The evil of slavery has not yet been redeemed primarily because only a remnant among the peoples has been willing to pay for it in the solid thought that is requisite for accurate diagnosis, or in the necessary labor like that of energetically altering one's habits of thought or of reorganizing institutional procedures, or in the suffering that accompanies the thought and labor. The impact of evil hurts, but unless someone is willing to receive its impact in order to redirect its energy, its direction cannot be changed toward good. To a great extent, the conspicuous spread of evil in the world measures not the impotence of God or the potency of evil, but common human laziness, reluctance to think, and unwillingness to endure pain.

My share in redemption pivots upon my attitude toward the past, and in particular upon whether I decide to use for good all that I have been given. Two hazards continually threaten that determination: the impulse to sentimentalize the past; and the tendency to force the process to a premature fulfilment.

Sentimentalism is emotion which, being separated from intelligence, lacks proportion, poise, and clarity. The sentimentalist may gloss over the sins of the past or exaggerate them; either way, he cannot act redemptively. If he underrates the sinfulness of the sin, he cannot take hold of more than a fraction of it. If he overemphasizes it, it defeats him. In both cases the sin becomes an illusion, and no illusion whether of grace or of nightmare contains enough substance to be instrumental in creating a new life. Honesty, accuracy, and justice are required to ensure that we are dealing with the facts of the sin.

The sins in question were genuinely damaging, and the facile judgment, "It was all for the best," is a lie. The sins can still be used for the best, but that is a matter of blood, tears, toil, and sweat, of the one Crucifixion and many crucifixions. They did not happen for the best. Because of them, we are forever maimed and the good for which God created us lies forever beyond our reach. He has indeed made another good available to us, in which our wounds are healed and our scars enhance the beauty of holiness. Nevertheless, the injury was real and permanent.

The opposite form of sentimentalism leads to denying that the sin can become an occasion for good. Thus I could very well have derived from my unsatisfactory relationship with my father the conclusion that all men are like that, and consequently fail to achieve a satisfactory relationship with any man. Or I could set other men in his place, and try to work out with them the ideal parent-child relationship which was not fulfilled in my childhood. Or I could allow myself to be trapped and then imprisoned by the past that has made me what I am, and measure all my accomplishments by what I think my father would have approved.

My past is not my prison unless I make it so, and I am entirely free to make of it an opportunity. Of course I do not always rise to the stature of the opportunities that are given me. I am perennially tempted to speed up the redemptive process, to determine by my own intelligence and decide by my own will what the good in the situation is, when I ought to be waiting for its inherent goodness to reveal itself. I keep pressing a moral on the story, squeezing the event to produce a meaning, crushing my perceptions into the mold of my present convictions. In my experience, however, the results of such endeavors are invariably commonplace and usually superficial — as if, for example, I had concluded that the lesson to be learned from the unanswerable question is that questions should be carefully asked and answered, or that parents should be patient with their children.

In contrast, God's redemption is always — again, in my experience — unexpected and radical: radical in the sense of going to the roots. It was not by taking thought that I came to see the problem of the past as not "Who was to blame for it?" but "What can be done with it?" — and the phrasing of the second question is critical. Not "What can I do?", which lays more stress on my power to act than is salutary here, but "What can be done?" And not "about it", which suggests manipulating the situation toward ends that are extraneous to it, but "with it", which implies finding what it already contains that might be of value. Nothing can be done about the sins of the past: there they are. But much can be done with them, because they carry within themselves the seeds of redemption. We cannot wrest goodness from them, but with patience, imagination, and accuracy, we can discover the goodness that is intrinsic to them, if only enough to enable the writing of a paragraph or the speaking of a single redemptive word.

2. *A Responsible Person*

While the problem of unanswerable questions arose more often and more urgently at home than at school or with my playmates, the problem of responsibility animated nearly every aspect of the world in which I lived, especially in the legalistic form, "What you earn, you get." If you have enough brains and study hard enough, you will be promoted to the next grade; if not, you will fail. If you are naughty, you will be punished; and if you are good, you will be rewarded. If you deserve love, you will be loved; if you are holy and righteous altogether, you will be saved — and fortunately God is loving, which in this context meant lenient.

I do not remember that the principle was ever stated so explicitly to me as a child, but it permeated my very bones. "Here are the rules, the harvest from centuries of experience. Submit to them and be happy, or disobey them and be unhappy. Because we, your elders, love you, we want you to be happy. Therefore we will see to it that you do submit, at least to the degree that we can control your behavior and govern your mind."

The pattern was rigidly mechanical in theory, although in practice it was considerably mellowed by admitting exceptions for individual differences in ability and need. It had some good for some of us who were subjected to it, because it did engender an acute sense of responsibility. I knew that if I had done wrong, I ought to be punished, not only as a method of reforming me but also as a proper requital. I ought to suffer for my wrong-doing whether the suffering did me any good or not, because it is only just for the sinner to bear part of the consequences of his sin. On the other hand, I became convinced that if I did right, I would possess the peace that inevitably proceeds from a clear conscience and a welcome in the community, and no higher recompense could be desired.

The moralistic features of responsibility were not greatly significant in themselves. It was what they manifested and made explicit that became of primary importance, and later enabled me to turn responsibility from a heavy weight on my shoulders into a firm support for my feet. To be responsible means to be fatefully involved. Punishment and reward alike are expressions of such fateful involvement, and therefore reassure the person that he belongs within the community. The bestowal and accept-ance of responsibility are tacit affirmations of mutual participa-tion.

For this reason, the most coercive ethical pronouncement in our family, so far as I was concerned, was: "There are some things that people like us just don't do." After that, the ques-tion "Why not?" rang thinly indeed, representing as it did an attempt to shift the discussion from the level of family loyalty to the level of private opinion. Wherever possible, of course, reasons for ethical norms should be given and were given to me. But behind the reasons always lay a judgment on the nature of man as a social being which might be intellectually defensible, but was the product of personal commitment rather than of demon-strated fact.

The sense of responsibility, of involvement, is in itself good. Like other good things, however, it can be used in the wrong way, and two of my gravest difficulties in reconciling myself with the past were the result of misunderstanding what I was respon-sible for, and of over-estimating the extent of my responsibility.

The first grew out of a proposition that I did not question while I was growing up, and now, after carefully examining it, still affirm with certain qualifications: that those who are good will be happy. Only to my sorrow, I interpreted the tense of the verb as referring to an immediate future or even to the present, and deduced an invalid consequent: that since to be good is to be happy, and I was responsible for my goodness or lack of it, therefore I was responsible for my emotional states. Moreover, I thought I could measure my goodness by my unhappiness or happiness, and I defined those two words in a crassly superficial way. In short, I established a direct and simple connection between volition and emotion, taking no account of external circumstances or historical events or a horde of other restrictions, and thereby fell into the second kind of trouble. "It's my fault if I am unhappy" led me to "I am in control of myself," which is one form of the deadly sin of pride.

True, it was unconscious pride, well masked under the humble realization that I managed myself very badly a good deal of the time. It was rooted in the glorious proposition that we are all members one of another. It represented a sturdy devotion to high principles and consistent effort to put them into practice. It was aimed toward improving myself so that I could serve others. None the less it was pride (and is, because I am far from being rid of it) because I was taking the responsibilities and the duties and the opportunities as if they belonged to me. I was seeing myself as necessary to the pattern of existence. God had no hands but my hands to do the work he had ordained for me, and if I did not accomplish that work, it would either not be accomplished or would fall as an additional burden upon somebody else. Since every person has his own unique quality, each is indispensable, and my contribution was needed to complete God's grand design for the world.

My pride was insidiously nurtured by sermons from clerics and laymen, by comments from teachers and associates, and by social and psychological pressures. Thanks to them, I learned to find satisfaction in doing a job well even though I disliked it, and to undertake unpleasant enterprises with reasonable grace — and let no one underestimate the value I place on the virtues of fine craftsmanship and outward cheerfulness. The source of these good things, however, was pride, and the sin of pride has a lovely face, her hands are deft in good works, and the death she bears in her body is swift to infect although slow to kill.

Pride tells us that her true name is self-respect, and that she is the mother of responsibility. With tears in her voice she points out the awful consequences of irresponsibility. Among church people, she speaks of our great significance to God as shown by his sacrifice on the cross for our redemption, until we glow with our self-importance. Or she shows forth a need in the community or world and persuades us that since no one else is engaged in correcting it, the sole hope for its mending lies in us. Following her lead, we hunt for activities that will make us or our unhappy neighbors feel useful, assuage our emptiness, and prove to ourselves that in truth we are still involved, still important.

Charles Williams broke the spell that pride had laid upon me, by his insistence that man is not necessary to God. "The web of created glory, exterior to Himself, is unnecessary to Himself. So the Divine Word need not have had a Mother, but exquisitely decreed that He would. So we need not love, but mightily decide that we will." Through my early training in responsibility, I had learned that I was fatefully involved with the world. Where I had gone wrong was in concluding that I *became* involved by accepting responsibility, so that if I were irresponsible or failed in my responsibilities I would become detached from the world. On the contrary, I was already involved to the hilt no matter what I did or did not do, and my basic responsibility lay in determining the manner of my involvement. I was a member of society, whether I abused my membership or used it creatively. I belonged to the world whether I rejected or accepted the world. I was loved whether I spurned love or embraced it. I was unnecessary to God and therefore unnecessary to my fellows and myself. And yet his love was so comprehensive that it included me, his faithfulness so enduring that he continued to sustain me, his acceptance of me so complete that he had died for me.

Such love, faith, and acceptance would be humanly intelligible if they were directed toward perfecting someone who was intrinsically precious, or if they represented an investment which might someday pay dividends by performing valuable service in the world, or even by pleasing my Maker as a satisfactory work of art pleases the artist. But a God who can raise up stones to be children of Abraham can get along very well without me. He who possesses in his Three Persons the plenitude of love will not be impoverished if I do not love him. *And yet* he loves me and all the other equally superfluous beings in all the rest of this superfluous world. He does not need our love — but he loves us. He does not need our help — but he lets us help. He has given us the sun and the moon and the stars, the rich earth and the clean air, and although we misuse his gifts, he does not rescind them. Also, of course, he has made wastelands and parasites, and he permits inconceivable horrors and ugliness even apart from man: wild animals burning alive in a forest fire started by lightning, fish tearing each others' living bodies apart for food. While we do not comprehend his reasons for allowing those dreadful things, they too are sustained by his incomprehensible love.

Nothing in the whole creation deserves such love, but we have it. Nothing we can do will repay such generosity, but he does not require us to recognize the giver in the gift, or to be grateful for the gift, as a condition for continuing to receive it. He has so made us, however, that we are hungry for love and thirsty for meaning: how can we not enjoy love and meaning when we receive them, as men who are dying of thirst and starvation savor water and bread? How can we not be grateful for what gives us joy?

My joy in being loved without a reason and beyond reason cried out for expression, for sharing. At the time I discovered love, I was still bound by silence, and in any case my awareness of such love was too frail to be spoken of, so whatever I did had to be done indirectly, through the ordinary round of writing, housework, and social activities. All the enterprises and most of the standards of my life under the régime of duty remained the same. Nothing changed except the reason for doing them. Earlier I had taken my place at the feast of life with the determination to eat because food is necessary for self-preservation, and self-preservation is necessary for service. Now I came eagerly, spurred by healthy hunger and pleasure in the company at the table. To do a job well in order to bolster my pride in fulfilling obligations was not the same as to do it well in order to show my love for my beloved. Even though the actions might look alike, the one possessed an inner grace, an elegance, that the other lacked. To take on a job as a matter of duty may be infinitely better than refusing to do it at all, but duty does not awake our imagination or skill or patience as love does. And only love can accurately guide us in determining whether we should undertake a particular job at all.

I have never been able to live at that level for very long at a time. The sense of gratitude and the emotion of joy are not my constant companions, and pride nearly always is. But though still a slave, no longer do I venerate my tyrant. My craving for recognition is like the craving of a drug addict for his narcotic, but to fight it directly serves only to focus my attention upon myself and therefore to nourish my pride. The motives impelling me from within are at best mixed and at worst deplorable, but in no case are they under my control.

What I can control are my intentions, the directions I choose to go, and through my intentions my motives receive — indirectly — their discipline. As George Macdonald once wrote:

> Troubled soul, thou art not bound to feel, but thou art bound to arise. God loves thee whether thou feelest or not. . . . Try not to feel good when thou art not good, but cry to Him who is good. . . . Then fold the arms of thy faith, and wait in quietness until light goes up in thy darkness. Fold the arms of thy Faith, I say, but not of thy Action: bethink thee of something that thou oughtest to do, and go and do it, if it be but the sweeping of a room, or the preparing of a meal, or a visit to a friend. Heed not thy feelings: Do thy work.

Doing our work will not save us from pride, or from the rebellion and impatience and despair that are the fruits of pride. But working, we incarnate our determination to express appropriately our involvement in the world, and thereby we implicitly acknowledge our gratitude to him who created the world in joy and for our joy. By responsibly involving ourselves in the world, we learn humility before its Lord.

In a limited but authentic sense, I have become irresponsible in my living: I do not take myself or my work as being ultimately serious or significant. Anything I do could be done equally well or better by someone else, and I rejoice in knowing it. In another sense, I have become infinitely responsible: because I belong to the world and to its creator, I am accountable to them and they to me, not from duty but in love.

3. *The Church and the Dispersion*

My whole life has been spent in the cultural milieu called Christendom. I have always belonged to a denomination of the Christian church and usually to a local congregation. I have frequently been active in church programs, and for half a dozen years "served" churches as a minister's wife. Therefore it is proper, and even necessary, to explain why the preceding and following description of my theological journey contains so little mention of churches.

The immediate answer is obvious but not very illuminating: that denominations and local institutions have directly contributed very little to my theological and religious development. What I received from them came indirectly for the most part, through their support of seminaries, Sunday schools at elementary levels, and the publishers of relevant books and journals. Why did I not avail myself of all their other resources? What factors of conceit or ignorance or waywardness or impatience barricaded me in loneliness when communities such as these were eager to give me their support and guidance and strength?

My dissatisfactions with ecclesiastical bodies did not stem from acquaintance with only one variety of Protestantism, or with Protestantism alone. At various times I have been closely associated with churches of the Presbyterian, Episcopalian, Quaker, Brethren, and United Church of Christ (Congregational) traditions, and in addition, I have had less intimate but still important relations with Baptist, Methodist, and Lutheran bodies, Roman Catholicism, and Judaism. Neither were my troubles the consequence of refusing to try seriously and for long periods to adapt myself to forms of activity, modes of thought, and styles of worship which the majority of church members and attenders appeared to find satisfactory. Bluntly, the root of my difficulty lay in my expectation, sometimes my demand, that the churches supply me with a nourishment, a stimulus, a foundation, which the local congregations and denominational bodies were apparently neither equipped to provide nor interested in providing.

I have been told more times than I can count, and more emphatically than I care to recall, that my attitude has no justification in theology or love because the Christian participates in a congregation in order to give and not to receive, to do something and not to get something. The church's function in the world (I am informed on excellent authority) is to be the Body of Christ, the redeeming community. In order to fulfil that task, it needs the faithful support of all its members, who should ask only what they can do for it, and never the supremely selfish and sterile question of what it can do for them. I was instructed that if I would break my self-will and learn to give without thought of reward, I would receive abundantly, but so long as I concentrated upon receiving, I was doomed to failure if not damned to perdition, and I had only myself to blame.

Such an interpretation of my relation to the church and the churches' relation to me would have been more persuasive if any local congregation I came across had been more flexible in defining what gifts it was willing to accept, and thus less emphatic in refusing such gifts as I had to offer. To take a small but entirely typical example: in one woman's group I was assigned to embroider a clothespin bag for a sale, and my timid request that I be permitted instead to knit socks for the mission that was to benefit from the sale was greeted so frigidly that I gave in, thinking it better to cooperate in a silly project than to insist on having my own way. It took me a whole winter of meetings to embroider that unspeakable clothespin bag, when I could have been knitting six pairs of good wool socks instead.

I have helped cheerfully — and efficiently — with cooking church dinners, attended innumerable quasi-social affairs, listened thoughtfully through interminable business meetings where my presence was required although my opinion would have been resented, and have taken on a wide variety of other activities for which I had no training, talent or inclination. Concurrently, the few things that I could do reasonably well, enjoyed doing, or felt were my specific vocation, have been considered of no value to these congregations, so that their members had no compunction about coercing me into the programs of their choice. In particular, my concern for the knowledge and worship of God was consistently, inexorably pushed aside in the interests of "church work".

No doubt their sort of "church work" has a place in the scheme of things, but my place is not doing that. No doubt the institution needs to be preserved into the future, but I have not been called to the vocation of institutional housekeeping, and while I am willing to contribute money for that estimable purpose, I am not willing to spend time or energy on it. No doubt the churches need all the help they can get, including mine, and always and everywhere the nature of the help proffered must be appropriate to the need, so that to give — let us say — dry bread to one who is dying of thirst is tantamount to refusing any help at all, and this is the charge that has been laid against me. In return, this is my charge against the churches.

If the congregations who incarnate the Body of Christ do not communicate to me the gospel and grace of God, where in God's name am I supposed to get them? If the churches do not support my vocation to learn and teach, where can I expect or hope to obtain backing? If I am not nourished by the community of believers, where can I find sustenance enough to do any work at all? Jesus said to his disciples, "Feed my sheep." The churches said, "Feed me." Jesus said, "Freely ye have received; freely give." The churches said, "Freely give; if you do not receive, it is your own fault."

The irony of the situation lay in the fact that most of my formal religious and theological instruction had been given me through the churches, but its net result was to separate me for many years from the very institutions which had nurtured me. So to speak, the disciples had brought me to their Lord, and I was consumed with eagerness to hear him. But while I tried to listen to him, his disciples were insisting that I turn my attention to them. They assured me that it was enough to hear them, and warned me that I could comprehend what he was saying directly to me only by means of their interpretations. They went further, to claim that unless his word to me resulted in my submission to them, it was not his word at all. My obedience to God was to be measured by my obedience to Catholic Peter or Protestant Paul or Orthodox John, or to Cranmer, Wesley, Luther, Calvin, Fox, popes, councils, or books.

I am not a church historian or a specialist in ecclesiology, but it seemed to me then and still seems that the church was made for man and not man for the church. God created the world before he placed the churches in the world. He sent his Son into the world before the Christian communities were established. The disciples were not first gathered into a society and then their Lord appeared among them; they first knew God in Christ Jesus and then discovered that they were members one of another. After he disappeared from their sight, they founded institutions to perpetuate his memory and the quality of life they had received from him. What first brought and then bound them together, however, was not agreement on general principles, or conformity of behavior, or reverence for a tradition, but something simpler, more direct, and more elemental: loyalty to the person whom they knew as the Son of God.

The Christian doctrine of creation implies that God is discernible in every shred of the world, supremely but not solely in his incarnate Son. The one thing needful, therefore, is to come to him by any means that are appropriate and convenient. The church is one of the means — the best for some people, not the best for others. Some whom God reaches by other means come finally to the church, or back to it as I did. But the priorities need to be kept clear, and all too often the churches' jealousy for their special position as continuing incarnations of the one Incarnation has produced a muddling of priorities. Since chronologically, God's revelation of himself in nature, history, and his Son preceded his revelation in officially organized congregations, it is not only legitimate but to be expected that many will seek and find God outside such congregations. Theologically, God is more important than nature or history or the church, and ideally the churches proclaim God, not themselves, to the world and welcome from the world all testimony the world can give about his appearance there. Practically, the churches I knew were almost unvarying in their refusal to listen to any word except what they had already appropriated, and then only if spoken in the dialect peculiar to themselves.

There can be no Christian life or faith without the Christian churches, for the excellent reason that historically it was the churches that preserved the records of Jesus' life and teaching. Presumably they might have been transmitted in some other way — Plato's ideas and influence have survived without the help of an Institute of Platonism — but in fact, that is how we do know about Jesus. To say, however, that there is no Christianity without the institution is not the same as to say that there can be no Christianity outside the institution, or that the word of the Lord cannot be heard, understood, and obeyed except within the framework of a local congregation.

In the years since I began my struggle to relate Christian theology to the Christian churches, it has become commonplace to differentiate between the faith and the institution, and to give priority to the faith over the institution. During the period of which I am writing, however, I found no one to support or enlighten me even to the extent of pointing out that in my rebellion against the ecclesiolatry of formulas and formalities, I was engaged in an indirect work of redemption, because the bitterness of my resentment impelled my search for evidence of God's activity in the secular world. My motive amounted to defiance; my intention was to prove the churches wrong in their claim that they were indispensable to God and man. Both the motive and the intention were destructive; the one constructive element in the situation was my acute sense that Jesus had more to him than was exhibited in the churches or by the pillars of those churches — not because they were imperfect disciples, but because they were or seemed indifferent to their Lord.

The God who knew me, and who had spoken to me through my dream, through C. S. Lewis, Dorothy Sayers, Charles Williams, my husband, and a thousand other remembered and forgotten ways, was far more visible to me outside the churches than within them. It was almost as if God revealed himself more openly where he was not named than where he was, in work not conducted under the aegis of any church, friendships based on interests other than common membership in a denomination, books with no ecclesiastical or even religious reference, social and political movements not instigated (and frequently not championed) by the churches, beauties of art and nature that the churches ignored. God was not at all confined in the churches, and the churches did not have a monopoly on his revelation. I was willing to concede reluctantly that a person could not be a Christian without church membership, but I insisted — and still insist — that he could be of Christ without it. Indeed it is not possible to be of Christ independently of a community — one cannot be a person apart from a community — but the community does not have to be ecclesiastical in form or connection.

The institutions I knew were based on doctrinal agreement or social conformity. They were solid and permanent. The groups in which God was most apparent to me were based on loyalties of various kinds: to the work we were undertaking, to the persons in the group, to the God who required of his people obedience but not unanimity or uniformity. They were fluid and temporary. Like Christ himself, they were natural bodies: born in nature, living out their time, dying when their members moved away or wandered apart, and raised from the dead as their erstwhile members spread into other groups. Communities like this, often composed of two or three who are gathered together, are not likely to survive very long. Neither did Jesus. They are vulnerable to error and divisiveness. So was he. They function within the world and speak the world's language. So did he: when God became man, he learned Aramaic.

These non-institutional incarnations of the one Incarnation belong to what I call "the Dispersion", taking the name from the word historians have given to the Jews living outside Palestine after the Babylonian Captivity, and to Christians who are isolated from churches or communities of their own faith. The type case is the isolated Christian living among pagans. By virtue of his knowledge and commitment, he is a member of a body from which he receives and to which he gives sustenance, although he may have direct contact with his fellow Christians only through the exchange of letters, or by means of books, prayers, and memories alone. There can be no Christianity without human intermediaries through whom the believer learns Christian history, doctrines, and practices. But a Robinson Crusoe, a prisoner in solitary confinement, or a companionless missionary does not forfeit his place and function in the Body of Christ because his union with it is maintained through the absent and the dead — who in their common Lord are neither absent nor dead.

Men and women whose individuality is rooted in God will inevitably come together into communities, and in any community which is consistently overshadowed by God in Christ, neither individualism (individuality cultivated for its own sake) nor conformism (the community cultivated for its own sake) will be a serious problem. Those who have been most actively engaged in the interaction between God and the world are the first and most forceful in emphasizing their need to replenish the abundance of their hearts by communion with others who share the same burden, labor to the same end, and obey the same Lord. They hunger and thirst for community, and when they find it — even in twos or threes — the Body of Christ is constituted in them as an indirect consequence. They are inwardly driven to gather together because only in the Gathering can they receive the substantial bread and wine that they must have as the completion of their relations with God and the world. If the local church does not give them daily bread, the Christian whom God has called to a vocation in the world is — I believe — required by his calling to go where he will receive it, without apology or blame.

It may have been my unique misfortune to live within and

among churches that seemed exclusively devoted to self-preservation, while the great preponderance of churches was in fact performing its proper function in proper ways. The fact remains that in my experience, abnormal or normal, the churches have not been willing to speak of God, and have not given signs of listening to him or to the world except within the straitened limits of what directly benefited them. Consequently, I have sought community elsewhere, and have found it within the Dispersion. Moreover, I was finally able to come to some sort of terms with the churches only after I had found nourishment outside them. Like the disciples, I discovered my Lord, and then my personal companions, and only after that the Gathered Community — the church.

4. *One Point of View*

I have no doubt but that my attitudes to the Gathered and Dispersed Communities will be taken as signal instances of that self-centeredness which permeates this book to its core. I started out with the selfish demand for a reason why I should live. I continued with the egocentric standard, "What rings true to me". I have described the process of theologizing in the most subjective of styles. Throughout my theology, as well as throughout my life, I have repeatedly neglected the objectively important in favor of the personally appealing, and calmly discarded neutral, universal propositions in favor of partisan opinions.

Yet I grew up in a world where selfishness was considered almost the worst of the sins, and selflessness was not only the norm for daily life but also the criterion for valid intellectual activity. The impartiality of the scientist and the judge, the detachment of the philosopher, the rigorous impersonality of scholarship, were treated as the supreme glories of the mind. My ears were not closed when the selfish were denounced and the selfless extolled. My heart was not so hardened that I preferred to be egocentric rather than exocentric. On the contrary, I yearned to lose myself in others or in activities or in God, in anything that would free me from selfishness, but I could find no way to escape.

In the fall of 1946, Emerson and I went to Pendle Hill, a Quaker center for study, so that he could finish the research for his doctoral dissertation on the history of the doctrine of the church in the Society of Friends. I worked half time in the office in part payment for our fees, and as a member of the community, I did my share of the work around the place. Apart from those responsibilities, however, I did nothing except what I wanted to do. We had just come from serving three churches where the minister's wife was expected to be a kind of assistant minister, and I was exceedingly weary of doing things because other people thought I ought to, or because I thought I ought to, or because I might jeopardize Emerson's career if I did not do them, or because of any other extrinsic pressure. So I established for myself the policy that during this one year, I would refuse all "opportunities for service" except those which I positively and spontaneously desired to accept, and when I did not know what I wanted to do or was merely passively willing to go along with a suggestion, I would wait before acting until I had determined what my real wants were.

From my remotest childhood, voices called: "You should be studying. You should attend the lecture. You should get some exercise. You should be doing something worthwhile." I ignored them. My conscience whispered: "You should plan a program of activities — any activities you like, but still a program. You ought to be involved in a socially useful project." I ignored it. My discipline for the year was to recover myself from the ore of parental, marital, and cultural influences in which I was embedded — and dissipated. So I sat. Sometimes I sat and knitted or read or wrote, and sometimes I sat and thought, but often I simply sat, wasting opportunities right and left while I watched the snow fall or the trees grow, and layer after layer of acquired tastes and habits of thought and patterns of response sloughed away.

I should like to report that by the end of that year, I had discovered what I did want, but that would be saying too much and too little. All I learned was to distinguish between what I spontaneously wanted and what I or others thought I should want. And I became less apologetic for wanting what I wanted. After we left Pendle Hill, I could no longer indulge in the luxury of doing only what I wanted to do, but at least I was partially free from the insidious variety of self-deception that results from confusing spontaneous reactions with artificial compulsions. Selfishness? It would be selfish to demand what I wanted. It was a step toward identity to discover what I wanted.

Moreover I learned — or rather, began to learn — that even

in a happy marriage, no two persons can be all in all to each other. While we were at Pendle Hill, my husband could not supply all my needs, not only because it was imperative for him to concentrate upon his dissertation in order to get a job the following year, but also because I needed something other than he could supply: a new light, a new refreshment, a different energy. For six years he had nourished me and I him until we had grown together; but we had also ingrown. Although his independent work as minister and scholar had supplemented his diet, adding flavor if nothing else, I had no equivalent resources. All the same, I was not feeling sorry for myself. It was nourishment I craved, not sympathy, and food to sustain my love for him, not another love to supplant it.

Selfishness? I suppose so — as a sick person is selfish for wanting treatment or a healthy person is selfish in wanting his dinner. But the categories of selfishness and unselfishness, so faithfully transmitted to me from my forebears and preached by my contemporaries, seemed to have almost no meaning any longer. I could not protect either my husband's freedom to work or our marriage except by tending to my own needs. As long as I battened on him, he was not only burdened by my demands but cramped by my style. Until I was a self in my own right, I had no self to give him. I could not become "selfless" except by first being "selfish". Years later, C. S. Lewis gave me the words that crystallized the idea I was groping for: "How can we meet [the gods] face to face till we have faces?" How could my husband and I meet each other face to face if my face were only a mirrored image of his, and his of mine? How can there be a plural, a "we", except as its components are singular?

The ideal of unselfishness that had been implanted in me was noble, sincere, high-minded, and founded on a doctrine of man that has nothing to recommend it except a transitory surface beauty. It prescribes a self-denial that amounts to dishonesty, and a self-abasement that amounts to suicide. Thus try as I might to minimize myself, if I left myself out of account in attending to my husband, I was neglecting an important factor in his environment. If I spoke with him at all, it was necessarily with my own voice and from my own mind. In order to retain a modicum of honesty and accuracy, I did not dare forget my individual self. On the contrary, I had to remember myself and keep calling attention to myself lest he (or anyone) suppose that I was claiming for my statements and actions more than a limited and tentative validity. So I reiterated "in my opinion" and "it seems to me" and "from my viewpoint" until I grew bored and impatient with such phrases, especially since the more I qualified what I said, the more inane the qualification sounded. What could I conceivably say or ask that did not have its source in my opinion? What can anyone say or ask that is not from his point of view? Even if I quoted, it was I who had chosen the quotation. The most authoritative statement by the wisest of men, backed with the most impressive evidence, still needs to be modified by "in my opinion" because he is, after all, a human being.

The uniqueness of our points of view is taken for granted in much of ordinary life. We have little difficulty in remembering that two persons looking at the same landscape or room or painting do not see it from quite the same angle. We tend to forget, however, that neither can two persons looking at the same idea see it from quite the same angle, and we cannot move as completely into each other's minds as we can move physically into another's footprints to perceive a view from his position. When we compare notes, the notes will mean very little unless we recognize the relation between our separate positions: you are standing above me; I am to your left. So until I could identify what position I was speaking from, until I had acknowledged the inevitable centrality of myself in my thinking and discovered not only that it was different from my husband's but precisely how it was different, and he did the same for himself and me, we could have no real meeting of minds on the levels where it mattered. Each had to establish his own point of view before he could do justice to the other's. We had to separate before we could come together on a level higher than that of undifferentiated fusion.

The centrifugal repudiation of the self is as damaging as the centripetal importunity of the self. As a corollary to this need for separation in union, it is as damaging to lay all one's burdens upon one other person as to refuse to share our burdens at all. No man can be a priest to his wife any more than he can adequately priest himself: he can indeed minister to her in myriads of other ways, but some sacerdotal functions, such as counseling and confession, apparently he cannot perform for her except perhaps in desperate emergencies. I am not sure why the roles of husband and priest, or husband and physician, or husband and friend, should be mutually exclusive. I am only certain that if all our needs could be met by any single person, he would become our god, and life or God or the evolutionary process has built into the universe a prohibition against such idolatry. Common observation and plain understanding indicate — to me, unmistakably — that the idolater destroys his idol and is destroyed by it with the same ruthless efficiency that characterized the extinction of the dinosaurs.

My husband could and did provide me with the bread of life, with daily bread and festal banquets to satisfy my hunger. He could not give me water or wine to quench my thirst. For me, the water of life is still just to sit. I do not contradict those who call that activity "contemplation", although I boggle at applying so exalted a word to so simple and natural an exercise. Once or twice in the twenty-odd years since we left Pendle Hill, I have had the chance to unwind slowly over a period of days, sinking at my own pace into the blessed stillness where all voices are silenced including my own. Never have I been permitted to drink deep of that water. The vacation ended or some other demand intervened. Usually I obtain no more than a sip of it: an uninterrupted hour when I am already partly unwound, a few minutes snatched as I run, the meditation which accompanies my writing and is an all but necessary preliminary to contemplation. So I am continually thirsty, and occasionally tormented by thirst.

I survive by the wine of my friendships. Long-during, temporary, intimate, casual, from them I have received (and sometimes, I think, have given) life. Wine is no substitute for water, and to the parched wine is less satisfying than water, but it is infinitely better than no liquid at all and has a delight and flavor of its own. Moreover, wine is no substitute for bread, or bread for wine or water.

The rhythm of thirst and hunger, of turning outward to friends and inward to each other, moves at its own speed and is not necessarily the same for my husband and me. Neither are we always nourished by the same food. One will need a change of activity when the other needs a change of pace. One will want conversation with friends at the same time that the other is eager for a little time alone with the other. Emerson and I have not mastered the intricacies of coordinating our separate rhythms, in part because both of us are still shackled by the traditional categories of selfishness and selflessness. Our thinking may have changed, but our thoughts have not yet converted our attitudes. Thus I still feel guilty when I beg off from a concert or visit in order just to sit quietly by myself: I still feel presumptuous in using, even in the privacy of my own mind, the words "to restore my soul". Surely, if I thought less of my "soul" and more of my husband, my "soul" would take care of itself. But it does not. Like the body, it has to be fed, and unless it is fed it makes an intolerable nuisance of itself. A person whose body is starving thinks incessantly of food, and only when his need has been satisfied can he work or play productively, or even sleep well. So the person whose soul is starved runs hither and thither scrounging for nourishment, or cries wearily, naggingly, for rest.

I do not agree with the conclusion that some people have drawn from similar data, that our first concern should be for ourselves, as if the alternatives still were only selfishness or unselfishness. I would say instead that our first concern should be to guard and enrich the total situation in which we find ourselves, and that our basic method should be to free each other and ourselves to become our own selves. The key categories — for me — are identity and integrity; the key process is liberation; and freedom is one and indivisible because we become free when we liberate others, and when we attain freedom for ourselves we become capable of bestowing it. The process is that of exchange, and it makes no difference whether we begin to exchange by giving or by receiving so long as we move within the pattern.

So, by the devious route of rebelling against an ancestral formula, I approached my present conclusion that the ultimate test of truth is its power to liberate. Statements, operations, relationships are verified or falsified as they free or enslave us. The truth makes us free; the truth is that which makes us free; and that which does in fact free us is the truth. But truth is not something we have. It is something we are in: partial truth if we are incompletely liberated, the whole truth if we are made completely free — not from ourselves or one another, but to become ourselves and so to unite with one another.

The ultimate enemies of freedom and therefore of truth are sin, which falsifies relationships by enslaving us, and death which destroys relationships. Thus in a human relation based on truth as I define it, there is need for effort to free the relation from whatever restricts the development of all the selves who are involved. The loving parent disciplines the child because it is not in laziness or bad temper that the child will grow into its own truth. The danger is that the parent will not discriminate between — for example — laziness on one hand, and a contemplative cast of mind or mental incapacity on the other, or between a temper tantrum whose source is vicious self-seeking and one symptomatic of an incipient illness or chronic frustration. In friendship and marriage, the loving discipline themselves and one another in subtler ways that their love opens to them, not trying to remake the beloved but to release him. And God disciplines us by methods that we cannot recognize until we recognize him, not punishing us because we have sinned but laboring to free us from our sins so that we may live, even now, within the truth and freedom for which he has created us.

The reconciliation of individual with individual, and of individuals with each other in community, is accomplished by a process in which nothing is lost but everything is transformed. The very definition of truth is changed: it is no longer a quality inherent in statements, to be tested by its power to withstand refutation, but a quality of relationships to be tested by its power to liberate. The standards of coherence, inclusiveness, and elegance are transformed from abstract concepts into concrete acts of integrity, community, and joy.

5. *"Whatever I Do Is Wrong"*

Thus far in the discussion of my coming to terms with the sins of my fathers, one element has been insufficiently stressed: my own sins and sin. I have done what I ought not to have done, and I have not done what I ought to have done, and I cannot look back on my previous history or examine my present condition without guilt for my major sins, as well as for the petty stupidities and spites that are sometimes more shameful than gross iniquities because they are so wretchedly undignified. The plaintive byword in my family, "Whatever I do is wrong," which was part an apology and part an expression of discouragement, is to me a literal truth. Whatever I do *is* wrong. More, it cannot help but be wrong because I am inherently both finite and sinful. Thus I do not merely commit sins upon occasion; my essential being is sinful, so that I have every reason to believe that I shall commit still more sins today, tomorrow, and the rest of my life.

The prospect is not pleasant, backward or forward, if one takes seriously the Christian doctrines of sin and judgment and eternal life. It is almost as bad as the meaninglessness I confronted when I began my theological journey. Since whatever I do is wrong, it would seem that I had better do as little as possible. But since inaction can also be wrong, what is there left? How can I face either my future or my past, not to mention my present? — especially since I strongly suspect that in taking the situation with as much gravity as I do, I have fallen again into the sin of pride, this time in the guise of scrupulosity.

Scrupulosity is not often regarded as a sin, in our day. We are likely to admire it as "having high ideals" or to rebuke it lightly as "perfectionism". Yet sin it is, the sin of being over-conscientious (as I am about keeping to a schedule for my writing?), over-fastidious (as in my rejection of images?), over-sensitive (as my anxiety over trivialities?), and over-weening (as in my attempts to perfect myself?). If I try to be perfect, either in the New Testament sense of fulfilling my intrinsic nature or in the ordinary sense of faultless, I succumb to arrogance or to despair. If I do not try, I become unprincipled and lazy. *Whatever* I do is wrong. To add force to the impact of my personal sinfulness, the world in which I live is so permeated with sin that the best of actions can lead to terrible evil. The life, death, and resurrection of Jesus have produced public and private abominations, and there must be many who have wished, in all intelligence and goodwill, that the Incarnation had never been inflicted upon man. At its divine zenith, good generates evil. How much more evil, then, am I producing even in those rare moments when I am doing my human best?

The answer to such problems was given me long before I felt the full weight of the burden of sin, and in relation not to sin but to another dreadful necessity. My father's death, when I was a junior in college, shook me badly. Some six weeks after returning to school, I gave up trying to find my own way out of my turmoil, and took to Dr. MacLeod the question whether I should give in to my emotions by letting myself go to pieces, or continue the exhausting effort to keep them under control.

Dr. MacLeod replied that there was a third possibility: "Accept it, and thank life for it."

I was so startled by his remark that I did not stop to ask him what he meant. The injunction, "Accept it," was obvious enough because I was already attempting frantically to accept the fact and all its implications. But "thank life for it"? Thank life for my father's death, for the cutting off of his life in the wealth of its maturity? Thank life for my family's and my deprivation? Be grateful that my father and I could never fulfil the personal (as contrasted with parent-child) relationship that we had barely begun to establish?

Twenty years later in the context of sin: can I be grateful that whatever I do is wrong? Should I thank life for the corruption of good and the perversion of joy that I contribute to life? Assuredly, it is not only impossible to do so; it is irrational and unreasonable to suggest it. Everything in nature and human nature declares against gratitude in such a context. Yet with a sound like the music of tremendous bells, it rings true to me.

It rang true then and it still rings true, truer than the voices of nature and human nature, and louder than the voices of reason or grief or repentance. I do not comprehend what those bells say. If I were asked what there is to be thankful for in my father's death, I would be hard put to answer in a way that did not ring falsely to my own ears. The only rejoinders that I have been given or have been able to concoct are unbearably trivial: for example, that it is better to die quickly at fifty than to suffer senile deterioration at eighty or to linger for years in pain; or that my father had finished the work God had created him for, so it was time for him to go; or that what is required is merely gratitude for his productive and satisfactory life. Such answers simply will not do. Similarly, I can find no justification for being thankful for my sins or the sins of the world, although I am very adept at excusing myself for behaving inexcusably. More nearly adequate is the proposal that we can rejoice because the outrages of sin and death contain potentialities for good. By means of them, we can learn compassion, humility, courage, patience, and other virtues. This is indeed one of the notes that the bells play, but only one, and it is in the middle range, not the highest or deepest tone.

So far, the nearest that I can come to suggesting what thanksgiving might mean in "Accept it, and thank life for it," is to quote a statement by Charles Williams: "Gratitude ... is love looking at the past" — with love defined here not as affection or approval, but as the determination to establish a redemptive interchange with the past, to maintain community with it. That is, I could look back in hatred and repudiate my responsibility for the past. Or I could look back in despair and deny the possibility of its redemption. Or I can look back in love, seeing the past in the ways that the lover sees his beloved.

The blindness of human lovers is proverbial. The lover perceives his (or her) beloved in a perfection wherein even her (or his) faults are caught up into a glory. His impatience is the manifestation of a divine hastening of the good to the Good. Her jealousy exhibits obedience to the divine command that we give ourselves wholly to Love. From the viewpoint of those who are not in love — who do not have their habitation in Love — the lover's vision is foolishness and scandal, but from the viewpoint of the lover, it is accurate perception of truth. And it may be that the lover's "blindness" is closer to what God sees than our judgments as neutral observers, meticulously dissociating the sinner from the sin. Furthermore, no sin is too gross to be included in love, whether by recognizing the sin as a perverted means for attaining a good end, or by the agonized confession that another's sins were responses to our sins so that we share a common life, or at the least, by acknowledging the sin to be a product of our God-given freedom, and therefore unimaginably grounded in Love.

Love does not look to the past to justify or condemn it, much less to erase memory or engender the sterile torments of the remorse that precludes repentance. What happened in the past is fact. Nothing except facts can be loved, and the only action Love can take toward a fact is to love it. I do not understand how even God can love some things, but I am not God, and as I confront these problems, I begin to wonder whether I understand anything at all. Because I do not understand, I cannot explain, but my failure in understanding does not prevent my seeing and adoring. Neither does it prevent me from attempting to understand and to obey.

Looking at the past gratefully, in love, produces repentance as inevitably as looking in love at another person produces humility. In that radiance, it is impossible not to see how we have outraged and degraded Love, and equally impossible not to see his steadfastness under our attacks. We have betrayed and deserted and falsified Love. But Love has not betrayed or deserted or falsified us. Therefore in turning from our sins we turn toward Love, and in loving we turn away from our sins. Either way, all is well, and the only alternative to these two motions lies in the disconsolate assertion that because we do not find love within ourselves, it does not and cannot exist independently of ourselves — a proposal that consigns us to the wanhope of the spiritually dying.

Repenting, we affirm the Love that upholds us whether we respond to it with love or hatred. Repenting, we take the sin into Love, secure in his capacity to love even where we cannot. Whether Omnipotent Love condescends to hate sins or sinners, I do not know. I do know that he commands me not to hate others' sins or my own, because hating them leads me to reject them, and whatever I reject I cannot carry into Love or give others to carry for me, and whatever is not taken into Love is unrepented and unforgiven. Usually I cannot do what I know I should do. The best I can manage is reluctant admission of the facts of sin, and dogged efforts to prevent my disgust at myself and my rage at others from obliterating my trust in Love's faithfulness. I obey, if at all, on a miserably low level. In trying to obey, however, I begin to understand dimly what this is all about.

By "taking the sin into Love," I mean loving the sin only in the sense of accepting it for what it is, not condoning it. Hatred does not accept. When we hate a sin or sinner, we become blind to the nature of evil itself, because evil is basically a degradation of the good. Behind the corruption of the created world lies the fact of the creation. Beyond the abuses of freedom we see the fact of freedom. Hating evil, we repudiate the creation and the freedom which are the ground from which evil grows. So understood, to love the sin is to acknowledge that it is rooted in good and therefore can be redeemed. The sins are not therefore less sinful, or the evil less evil: indeed, their depravity is emphasized by the contrast between what is and what should have been. Bringing sin and love together, we cannot evade the smallest particle of sin's abomination, or underestimate the effort that will be required for its redemption.

As students of literature and mathematics and music learn their subjects by practising them, so I learn about love by loving, and like students in other areas, I must begin at the beginning.

Loving sinners and sins belongs to an advanced course, not an introductory one, and I have not yet mastered the elementary procedures of loving the persons I already like. For a long time I thought it was enough to cultivate my natural fondness for certain persons, and I called this "love", but it is not — at least, it is not love in the Christian sense. Instead, I am called to recognize that my beloved ones are not mine but God's, and that my joy in them is God's gift through them. With my friends, it is comparatively easy to find the divine gift, and a delight to acknowledge in them my debt to God. But I tried to skip that chapter in the textbook. I attempted vigorously to love my enemies and myself before I knew how to love God or my friends and before I knew that the most intense and enduring natural attractions are only images of the divine Love and cannot substitute for the reality they image. Nature cannot replace God, even though God's love is not available to man except by means of our natural loves. The spirit is given and received by its incarnation in the letter.

In any field, the grasp of a principle can precede, perhaps by years, the ability to apply it. One of the things which I can envision and can occasionally practise is that when the admission, "Whatever I do is wrong," is spoken to God, it becomes an affirmation of joy and peace. Then, and then only, the unconditional confession of sin is taken up into the Love which acts within my sin to counteract it, and by means of my sin. Of course whatever I do is wrong. And although I cannot rejoice in my sins, I can rejoice unstintingly in the power of Love to act through me and through them, whether I know it or not, and whether I am trying to cooperate with him or to obstruct him. My sin and sins could destroy me; they cannot diminish him. They can prevent my accepting his love, but not his giving it. Since he can forgive my sins and use them for his own purposes, I can look at them gratefully, enlightened by his incomprehensible love.

To anyone who has been educated from infancy to believe that he is morally bound to do his very best to be good, the admonition that he should be content to be a sinner sounds like the ultimate in degeneration. But for those of us who are paralyzed with fear of doing the wrong thing, and with guilt for having done so many wrong things, any weaker precept would be inadequate. We are in no particular danger of leaping to the other extreme of moral indifference. To borrow Dante's metaphor, we need the bridle, but even after being broken to it, we are unlikely to need the spur for correcting sloth or unscrupulousness. The proud sin of scrupulosity is not so easily vanquished as all that, even though temporarily she may disguise herself in the false humility of a strident unconcern, declaring that if she cannot have perfect goodness, she will refuse the good she might have.

Being content to be a sinner does not imply being satisfied with our sins or desiring to sin. It does check our rebellion against the facts of sin, and counteracts the despair that follows rebellion. It gives us courage to do what we can, secure in the conviction that God will perfect the good in it and redeem the evil, and it teaches us love and faith, thereby preparing us to practise — and ultimately to understand — the virtue of hope.

chapter seven

THE VIRTUE OF HOPE

Gratitude is a necessity of all life; it is love looking at the past as faith is love intending the future, and hope is the motion of the shy consciousness of love in the present self...
CHARLES WILLIAMS, *He Came Down from Heaven*

When all the obscurities have been illuminated and all the evils redeemed, the theologian's work is still not finished. There remains a class of questions which for me is the most difficult of all: the reconciliation of great opposing glories: of faith with knowledge, the ideal with the real, reason with emotion, mind with matter, and time with eternity. I suspect that the longing for such a reconciliation is one of the roots of the widespread desire for a supernatural heaven. Since the union of seemingly incompatible perfections is not accomplished on this earth, we project its fulfilment into a world to come. Christianity, however, does not restrict heaven and eternity to the future. It says that the reconciliations of heaven are available now. We can have our heaven on earth, and the Christian hope is not so much *for* something that will come, as *in* something that is now going on. Thus for the Christian, hope is only secondarily an emotion to be enjoyed. Primarily it is a virtue to be practised. It does not concentrate upon a future in time, but upon the timeless reality of the eternal present.

But our access to eternity, and therefore to hope, is through time. So before considering the eternal present, it will be necessary to sketch my temporal present in more detail than has hitherto been required.

1. *The Field of Battle*

For reasons of brevity and structural clarity, the narrative so far has dealt mainly with personal crises and crucial experiments, and the style of writing has reflected the drama of those critical moments. But to recount only the dramatic action, without reference to the setting of the stage, may create the dangerously false impression that the theological life is more uniformly exciting than in fact it is.

The impression is dangerous because when the unwary find that it is in most respects a very commonplace life indeed, they may all too easily give up the enterprise as a bad job, or set themselves to the self-defeating labor of trying to conjure up "appropriate" emotions and incidents. Theology is like every other vocation, including parenthood, politics, art, science, and warfare, in offering its practitioners long periods of steady, uninspired toil, frequent intervals of boredom or mere waiting, and only occasionally the splendor of a vision or the flaming tension of an assault. A particular battle may be the decisive encounter in a major war, but the ordinary sun shines above it; ordinary soil or sand or water or air constitutes the battlefield; the combatants once lived ordinary lives; and between their engagements, they still function in ordinary ways.

For the most part, my outward and inward lives are not much different from those of any other middle-aged, middle class, Middle Western housewife who is childless or whose children are not living at home, and who has a half-time job. I spend four hours a day, six days a week, at my writing desk or typewriter. In general, the rest of the time I am occupied with completely unspectacular household, social, and public affairs. Even in times of high religious or theological intensity, the routines of cooking and dishwashing, meetings and concerts, keeping accounts and visiting with friends, form a substratum that provides me with relief, distraction, and continuity for my theological work.

I do not ordinarily live on the heights with which this book is largely concerned. I do not strain to find theological meanings in what I do and observe. I do not exert myself to practise the presence of God. I rarely talk about theological or religious affairs directly unless somebody else brings the subject up. I attend services of worship with only fair regularity, and participate in ecclesiastically sponsored meetings only on the infrequent occasions when I am invited to lecture to a church group. Much of the time I spend writing goes into matters of organization and craftsmanship that are almost identical with those that are faced by writers on any other subject, from a journalist's report on a political meeting to a poet's creation of a song.

Like any other person who is serious about his job, however, I half unconsciously notice ideas and information that are immediately relevant to what I am doing. Therefore I naturally tend to perceive theological implications in whatever I am engaged in, although without deliberately trying to do so. As the economist is swift to see the economic implications in public affairs, the physician automatically notices signs of health and disease in those he meets, and the artist notices the line, mass, and color of what he sees, so I remark that a movie reflects a dualistic view of reality, or a piece of legislation presupposes a more optimistic doctrine of man than I think the facts will warrant, or a particular argument should be continued later because an important epistemological issue was not resolved. I think theologically as a devoted mother thinks maternally, by reflex, because this is where her concerns are centered. As Michael Innes writes: "Have you ever talked to crack newspapermen? They'll tell you that the big things come not through hunting but simply through carrying round a certain state of mind."

Meanwhile — what of the larger world outside my little household and neighborhood? I have lived through two world wars and several smaller ones, a major depression, the onset of the Atomic Age, riots, assassinations, cultural revolutions, brutalities and injustices galore, none of which appear to have influenced my theological development as outlined in this book. Where have I been all those years? How can I possibly justify my failure to become actively involved in the great events of my time, and with my suffering, struggling kindred all over the world?

Persons vary as widely in their personal responsiveness to public movements as they do in their biological responsiveness to physical events. One person will be susceptible to a virus that another is immune to; one will thrive on a food that the other cannot digest. Likewise, one person will be decisively affected in his personal growth by a political or economic change that scarcely touches another on that level of his existence. A person may indeed be compelled by a war or depression to alter his whole manner of living, without noticeable alteration of his general world view or attitudes toward the world.

We grow as we can and must. Our capacities, our interests, our opportunities, impel us in different directions. We are nourished by different foods and called to different vocations. And the highest form of the religious life — at least according to Christianity — is not action, or even theology or worship, but obedience to the calls that we individually receive.

I have been told in so many words that I should not be doing what I am doing, and told in effect that the theological and contemplative life is a luxury which mankind cannot afford in these hours of peril. I am informed that my work is irrelevant and escapist, that it tacitly encourages those who would prohibit Christians and Christian organizations from engaging in political and social enterprises, and that I am not living in the Twentieth Century. Such strictures worry me, both because they may be correct, and because they imply that obedience will result in uniformity rather than diversity. Yet if the Lord is indeed efficient as well as omnipotent, presumably we can trust him to supplement social activists with an occasional contemplative, and counterbalance the theologian with an appropriate number of civic leaders.

I have not been called to public activity, and I say this while admitting that what I fondly entitle "my vocation" may be no more than a rationalization for laziness, cowardice, social irresponsibility, or any other of a multitude of sins. Clearly, many of the evils in our social structure can be vanquished only by massive action on the part of governments and large private organizations. Such movements need the active support of every citizen, including me. Intelligent support calls not only for acquiring information, but also for sizable contributions of time, effort, and money. The needs are critical and urgent, but I am not studying them closely, or "giving until it hurts" in those areas.

Also, however, there are needs of many kinds, and the important ones — such as for equal educational opportunity — cannot be met by a unilateral effort. The situation of inequality must be approached from a number of directions, including not only federal and state legislation, but the individual changes of attitude which are produced only by slow, patient, face to face confrontations. Neither strategy will succeed alone, and each strategy requires a different set of qualifications to implement it.

The specific job to which I have been called — or which I

have chosen — is that of helping to develop human beings into responsible persons. As a corollary, I am fighting against all those elements and forces in individuals and societies which tend toward depersonalizing man. In the battle for man-as-person, my special rôle is to build bridges between laymen and theologians by interpreting theology to laymen, and the laity to the theological community.

I cannot simultaneously build bridges and man a machine gun, stand sentry duty and lead patrols against the enemy. Whether my job is relatively important or unimportant in the total scheme of things is beside the point. Naturally I like to think of it as having more than temporary and local value, but while I can see part of the field of battle, I cannot see the overall plan of battle, so I do not know. Nor is there any need for me to know. I have been given one particular responsibility. I am immeasurably glad that others are doing what I am not called to do. I hope they will not scorn me if I do not march with them. And I pray that I will refuse the temptation to abandon my own job when they press me to join their crusades.

The battle against depersonalization constitutes only one phase of the war against evil. The pencil constitutes only one weapon in the arsenal. I need the support of others; it is reasonable to suppose that they might be able to use the help I can give. I am not gravely concerned when others claim that their jobs are more important than mine, their sector the decisive one, their functions higher and more demanding. In the pattern which C. S. Lewis and Charles Williams call "the Great Dance", every motion is essential and therefore in some sense the focus for all others. What does disturb me is the mounting pressure from those who clamor, "Because my vocation is critically significant, you should abandon your own and come and serve mine," or worse, "Because mine is a valid expression of social responsibility or Christian commitment or the true nature of man, therefore yours is invalid." They do not invite others to join them, as they legitimately might; directly or indirectly, they seek to coerce.

The sentry's post is mocked by calling it an ivory tower, and the sentry is made to feel guilty for following his orders faithfully: the argument goes, "He that is not with us on the battlefield is against us." The strategist at headquarters discounts the reports that come to him from the field: "All those fellows exaggerate." The radical of the right or left cries out, "If you

don't do things my way, I'll break the system," or in the brilliant-
ly expressive phrase, "I'll drag you kicking and screaming into
the future." We are oppressed by an all-or-nothing mood that
threatens to petrify into an all or nothing rule. We are all supposed to be "modern" and "young". "Behold, we make all
things new."

Being neither a historian nor a seer, I find the label "modern"
— so used — not very illuminating, and the attempts to anticipate
the future not very convincing. I do find, on my doorstep, persons
of all ages who in one way or another are trying to avoid the
guillotine or to remedy its effects: the separation of intellect from
passion, the individual from society, parents from children, action
from contemplation. For me and for some of them, the image of
the guillotined man conveys the disintegrity of our present world
more vividly than any other. And my neck also is ringed with
the red line which shows that the head is set on top of the
shoulders, but that the blood vessels, nerves, muscles, and bones
which should connect them have been severed. At least, however, I know what has happened, and I will not accept the situation as hopeless for myself or any other.

Our fight against the guillotine and its effects must be fought
person by person. Some battles can be waged by collective action; this one cannot be. Therefore when I focus my energies
upon individual persons rather than social revolutions, or write
in the hope of touching individuals rather than swaying a crowd,
I have not relegated myself to a position above the battle, but am
simply engaging in it on another front.

Most of the people I know are in situations much like mine;
I have undertaken to defend my own vocation for the sake of
supporting them in theirs. They also are harassed by incessant
solicitations for help, although none of us has the time or the
inner resources to comply with even a small fraction of them.
They also are unnecessarily handicapped in doing their proper
work by a burden of guilt imposed upon them by partisans with
a one-track mind. Certainly we should not deafen ourselves to
the demands of the zealots. Neither should we submit to their
importunities if in so doing we betray the trust that has been
placed in our hands. It is incumbent upon all of us to differentiate between enemy and ally, and to encourage those allies
who are fighting on other fronts, whether in slums or laboratories, whether against other forms of sin, and whether by personal

encounters or by legislation, public relations, and political campaign. The battlefront is wide enough, the strategy complex enough, that every skill can be used and every function is indispensable.

2. *The Sense of Touch*

I can write letters on the typewriter, but not articles, books, my little unpublished parables, or the unpublishable tirades in which I fight certain of my extremely private battles. So strong is this proclivity that when my right arm was nearly disabled for a time because of a pinched nerve, I had to learn to write with my left hand or remain dumb.

Writing by hand is slow compared with brushing the keys on an electric typewriter, and the results of my longhand are not always legible. There are few practical justifications for clinging to such an archaic procedure. There is, however, a sound personal reason — or perhaps rationalization — which has to do with the age-old problem of the relation between the letter and the spirit, the concrete and the abstract.

I am continually working with abstractions: concepts, principles, symbols and their referents, mental structures, systems of thought, words, things that can be envisioned but not seen, imagined but not touched. As long as they stay within my mind, they are immaculate but sterile. Their fruition depends upon translating the spirit into the letter. The word must be spoken and heard, or written and read, if it is to live. The spirit must be physically embodied. And somehow, for me, the spirit moves more freely in the crude physical labor of forming characters with a pencil than by interposing a machine between my fingers and the paper. It is as if the living word and spirit, idea and image, need for their consummation not simply a material vehicle, but a vehicle of living flesh.

At best, the body seems to corrupt the spirit. The word fails to communicate the idea adequately; the symbol conceals its referent; I cannot, whether in language or actions, exhibit faithfully the glory I have seen. And I am not uniquely incompetent in that respect. If we keep our ethical principles — as of honesty and justice — sufficiently modest, we can live up to them, but we cannot live up to the highest we can see. Our deficiencies, or the deficiencies of society, or "the sheer, damned cussedness of things," undercut our efforts so consistently that we finally surrender our visions of perfection except as signs indicating the general direction we would like to go. "Ideal" comes to mean "impractical", and "idealist" becomes a contemptuous predicate.

Characteristically, I found my clue to the relation between the ideal and the real in a place where I was not looking for it. The occasion for the discovery was the writing of this book, which has required me to shift rapidly and frequently between theological principles and historical events. During that process, I have come to believe that the truths which are laid bare by abstraction are of secondary importance. Their validity may be irrefutable, but their power is dead.

Even supposing that a general proposition such as "All men are mortal" is true in the sense that it could be completely verified and could not be falsified, it has no meaning except in its relations with other statements of the same aseptic kind. Together, such abstractions constitute a highly sophisticated and sometimes exquisitely beautiful realm of discourse, but it is created by dissecting from life a carefully selected group of elements, and it has — at its best — every merit except the crucial one of vitality. It is the world of the primary color on the palette and the pure chemicals in the laboratory, obtained by refining the desired fractions from the heterogeneous substances found in nature. I am not denying either the validity or the utility of abstractions. I am proposing that unless the pure forms that have been extrapolated from life are re-interpolated into life, they are inert and meaningless. Thus the proposition "All men are mortal" is a distillation from experience, but it has nothing to do with the terrified cry, "I am dying!"

The incompatibility of the rational proposition and the emotional outburst is displayed most clearly when we try to translate one into the other. To subtract the dimension of passion from "I am dying!" annihilates the frame of reference, the "I" who produced the cry, so that it is stripped of its meaning — which is not rational. Conversely, if we add the dimension of passion to the abstract statement, we destroy the lucidity which is the prime justification for abstract thought. When the detached intellect becomes impregnated with the confusion, the immediacy, and the contingency of actual events occurring in actual history to actual persons, its own frame of reference is corrupted and the generalization loses its deductive certainty. If the two statements are brought together in such a way that "All men are mortal" effectively gives form to "I am dying!", the abstraction is no longer trivial: it has been transformed into the sufferer's proclamation of his community with all other men who are likewise dying.

So doing, however, the abstraction is changed into something quite different. "All men are mortal" does not mean that we are members one of another through our common mortality. The meaning and function of the statement have been compromised. Something is gained by such a union: under the illumination of ardent experience, the lifeless assertion is transfused with triumphant life, and in the light of the abstraction, the unreflective chaos is ordered into a new creation. But something also is lost. The union of ideal principle with material history effects so violent a change in both that we are reminded again of our chronic inability to apply our principles without compromising their purity, or to retain their purity without reducing them to impotence. Separately, the abstract idea is sterile and life is wantonly prolific, but together they are changed. Whatever we do, we appear to violate one or the other.

I belong to a culture in which science, religion, and common sense generally agree in separating the abstract ideal from the concrete real, and in alternately damning the one for being impractical and the other for being irrational. "Absolute truth" is conceived of as belonging to the realm of pure thought, and "absolute goodness" as undefiled by the faintest whisper of expediency, while "absolute beauty" has been spiritualized out of any meaning the phrase may once have had. I am sufficiently imbued with my culture that I cannot wholly escape those connotations, but I have come to believe that the very concepts of absolute truth, goodness, and beauty are radically imperfect specifically because they are abstract, detached, discarnate, pure. As a corollary, I believe that no ideal or idea or virtue becomes absolute until it is embodied in particular persons and events.

On this ground, we are not weakly compromising our ideals when we oppose high-minded legislation that cannot be enforced. On the contrary, we are thereby holding fast to the embodiment of truth against the world's unceasing pressure to make the truth irrelevant and ineffective by disembodying it. "Absolute" or "ideal" love becomes, by my definition, that love which is practised, no matter how hesitantly or clumsily. When we set "pure" justice and "pure" mercy against each other, we are treating them like pure chemical compounds. Sealing them from interaction, we may ensure their freedom from contamination, but we destroy their potency except as a theoretical possibility: we do not allow them to be potent. In short, I have concluded that the ideal is to be identified not with ideas but with action. The absolute is perceived not by intelligence or imagination but by the sense of touch, the most remote by means of the most immediate.

Of all our senses, the least developed in our day is the sense of touch. Children are brought up by the slogan, "Look — don't touch." Adults may shake hands and women may touch cheeks, but any other bodily contact is liable to be interpreted as a sexual advance or response, and as such is a potential cause for scandal. Husbands and wives may give each other the depth of reassurance that cannot be conveyed except by the contact of body with body, but parents are discouraged from caressing their own children, friends from holding hands, and priests from the laying on of hands for solace or blessing. We know one another at a distance by sight and hearing, but not by the immediate pressure that resists and supports us mentally as well as physically. Touch is indeed the most intimate of the senses, but not all intimacy is sexual in motivation, purpose, or implicit reference. Neither our physical nor our personal lives are bounded by our sexual functions, and all our other functions are starved when the exchange of touch is permitted only within an authorized sexual context. Our most interior, most spiritual selves are brought to life by touch and not by words or sounds or sight. We can feel the presence of God in our bodies when we do not know him with our minds.

It was with considerable surprise that I saw my chain of reasoning about abstract propositions and concrete action leading me straight to the Christian doctrine of incarnation, with its implication that the immaculate purity of the absolute is not violated but fulfilled by the transition from thought to touch. The discarnate truths of formal propositions and doctrinal models — valuable though they may be as means — are ultimately not only secondary but second-rate, because the truth in its fullness — absolute truth — is inextricably bound with the way and the life.

Further, our highly refined, abstract ideas about truth, goodness, and beauty — or faith, hope, and love — are as deadly to us as pure oxygen. "The first thing a principle does — if it is really a principle — is to kill somebody," wrote Dorothy Sayers in *Gaudy Night,* which is a masterly exposition of that text and of its opposite: the equally devastating consequences of being unprincipled, or trying to live (as it were) without oxygen. Without oxygen in combination with other elements, life as we know it on our planet would cease within minutes; without moral principles and intellectual ideas, our societies would swiftly die. But in their purified and isolated form, neither oxygen nor principles are useful except for occasional specialized purposes. It is in their combination with other substances that they become life-giving.

It follows that no idea, doctrine, or virtue will be Christian until it is incarnate in flesh. Strictly speaking, I can no longer accept any verbal description or definition of love as Christian, although certain concepts of love become Christian when they are acted upon. Similarly, I seriously doubt that there is any such thing as a Christian theology. Rather, there seem to be only the theologies of Christians, who are identifiable by various more or less conspicuous similarities, above all by their emphasis upon incarnating the spirit in "the holy and glorious flesh". I sometimes think that the deadliest sin for the Christian is to be impractical: to refuse or not to know the conditions that must be met before incarnation can occur, because that would be a denial of both the creation and the method by which God is redeeming his creation — or has redeemed it.

My belief in the Christian doctrine of incarnation, and in the God who chose to be Incarnate, is derived from my conviction that love and truth and goodness and faith are more nearly perfected in *any* embodiment than in *any* abstract idea. The personal choice to respond impersonally can itself be good and beautiful, and can lead to truth and love, on those occasions when impersonality is adequate to a limited and temporary situation, as in casting accounts or building an engine or analyzing a word. But we dare not confuse any such particular situation with the human situation, which is incarnational.

Necessarily, therefore, all our judgments must be relative because they are products of the incarnate relations that support the judging person. We cannot know things as they are; we know them only as we can, only as we are related to them and they to us in action and touch. Deep within ourselves, however, we hunger to know if we have achieved a relation that is right not only in relation to ourselves, but universally and eternally right. What is the final truth, the ultimate judgment, the last thing, the *eschaton?* When shall we possess or be possessed by certainty? Under what conditions shall we know perfect truth and beauty, and how will they know us? Or is our hunger never to be satisfied? Are we never to learn if we were wrong or right, but to be dropped soundlessly into oblivion? If truth is reached by incarnation, we shall know the answers to such questions when we have completely lived them — that is, when we die. But we can glimpse some of the possibilities in our preliminary dying, when those whom we love have died.

3. *The Edge of the Volcano*

The United States Marines invaded Iwo Jima on February 19, 1945. The first dispatches in the Topeka newspapers named my brother Jim and identified his part in the invasion. At that time, I was working in an office as a typist, and after seeing that morning paper, I returned to my assignment with — I suppose — a normally calm appearance, but feeling as if I had suddenly been transported to the edge of a volcano, to the tremulous rim of a crater seething with fire. As the day went on and the pages of finished typescript piled up on my desk, I became increasingly convinced that my initial image of the volcano accurately portrayed my situation in every respect except one. I had not been suddenly transported to that precarious position. Instead, this was where I had always been living, although I had never before realized it. The ground under my feet had never been solid. I had never in my life been safe.

Twelve days later my brother was dead, killed in action by a sniper's bullet through his heart.

Five months later Hiroshima was destroyed by the bomb that inaugurated the Atomic Age.

Since then, most of the world has learned what I discovered when I knew that Jim had gone into combat: that we are all living on the edge of a volcano, and always have been. Every motion, every abstention from motion, is loaded with immediate peril. Every instant carries a new threat. An infinitesimal slip of a mind or hand can annihilate all life as we know it. But there is nothing new about that condition apart from our perception of it — and many, of course, learned it far sooner than

The Virtue of Hope

I. Once we may have been blind; now we see that the ends of the earth are upon us.

In this extremity, what do we have to hope in, to hope for? The question is urgent. It is said that while there is life, there is hope, so that as long as my mother, my sister, and I did not know of Jim's death, we could hope for his survival; when we learned of it, we could no longer hope either for him or for ourselves. As long as nuclear warfare or a nuclear accident does not destroy life on our planet, we can hope that nothing of the kind will occur. But if it does, what hope can we have in the numbered hours before we painfully die?

The easy answer is that our hope is in the Lord who made heaven and earth, and in whom we shall continue after death to live and move and have our being. Yet no words grate more harshly on our ears when our future contains nothing except the intolerable presence of an absence, or when we are too anguished or weary or tortured to want a future in this life or any other. To the hopeless, the injunction to hope is more than merely futile: it is insulting. It denies the reality of despair, and therefore of the person in despair.

How we approach the problem of hope depends upon whether we take the word "hope" in its common or its Christian sense. The dictionaries I have consulted all define hope as desire and expectation — that is, as implying an emotional state when events hold promise of improvement or at least of not changing for the worse. Christianity, however, has traditionally defined hope as a virtue, like faith and love, which can be practiced whether we feel like it or not, and which does not supplant our natural impulses but transforms them. Thus the emotion of hoping in a future fulfilment is a natural preliminary to exercising the Christian discipline of hope.

The parallel between the Christian treatment of hope, and its treatment of faith and love, is exact. The customary secular meaning of faith is the feeling of security, of love is the feeling of affection, and of hope is the feeling of anticipation. As feelings, they may be virtuous in the sense of being praiseworthy, but they do not become virtues in the strict sense until they are the products of deliberate choice and have become habitual forms of response — attitudes rather than impulses. We cannot choose what emotions we shall have: they are involuntary reactions which we can cultivate or repress, acknowledge or disguise, and follow or disregard in our actions, but we cannot directly generate or change our emotional states by acts of will. For that reason, the virtues must refer not to spontaneous feelings, but to acts that can be undertaken regardless of our emotions and of the motives with which our emotions are associated.

Our motives, those forces in the innermost self that compel us from within, are too deeply buried for us to know them with certainty, too subtle for us to analyze precisely, too violent for us to control. We can, however, control our intentions, the ends toward which we direct those motivating forces. As the water from an artesian well, driven by subterranean pressures, can be channeled by a pipe, so our motives can be directed by our deliberately chosen intentions. The illustration must not be carried too far, because the interplay of motive and intention, and of both with intelligence and emotion, is more complex than can be expressed by elementary hydraulics. Indirectly, though not directly, intentions may in time work backward upon the emotions, and perhaps even upon motives, until ultimately the will to do good to one's enemy may result in liking him; the decision to act upon what we have decided to believe may result in a most profound and far-reaching sense of security; and the resolution to accept life as a gift from God may result in the confident expectation of good. Or they may not.

The virtues can be practiced not only in the absence of appropriate emotional concomitants, but also in the presence of inappropriate ones. How we feel toward the future depends upon more or less transient physiological states, obscure attractions and repulsions whose sources we cannot locate, social and psychological influences, and a host of other factors, most of them erratic in their effects and few of them, if any, responsive to our commands. But how we behave in the present does not have to depend upon how we feel about the future, any more than politeness toward our neighbor must depend upon our affection for him. Our actions can represent the steady conviction that the future is in God's hands, and our steadfast determination to acknowledge his support in the present. So doing, we need not — and certainly should not — pretend to ourselves that we feel the emotion of hope when it is lacking. Dishonesty and inaccuracy play no part in practicing any virtue. All we need to do is to act according to our deliberate commitments rather than our transitory impulses.

In other areas, we take for granted such an ordering of our lives. Most breadwinners do not succumb to every desire for a day of fishing. Most school children attend their classes regularly even if they do not feel like it. Most marriages are held together by something more than whim. The subordination of feeling to reason is the same with respect to faith, hope, and love. It is one thing spontaneously to look ahead to the fulfilment of an aspiration, and something entirely different to work faithfully toward that fulfilment. The crucial question is not what we feel but what we intend, and whether we are serious enough about our intentions to act on them.

The virtue of hope is a stable attitude resulting from perseverance in the decision to interpret events as belonging to a meaningful pattern rather than as capricious sequences. In the context of Christian faith, to hope is to affirm the presence of God in whatever happens, and the power of God to use creatively whatever happens. Thus hope is allied to faith, which is our choice of the basis on which we shall act, and to love, which is our choice to live in community. The intention to know all things coherently, and to live with all things freely, is accompanied and enlivened by the intention to embrace all things joyously, to celebrate reconciliation.

Because the Christian places his hope in the God who is with him now, his hope is justified in the moment of his hoping. He does not need to wait for events to prove him right in being hopeful: his rightness lies in the act that establishes his habitation in joy. And I do not mean by "joy" that his emotions are pleasant, but that he affirms God's presence in all things and moves swiftly to honor God in all that occurs. His praise may ring with laughter or be muttered between sobs: what counts is his intention to glorify God, and his determination not to be overcome by evil because it, like ourselves, is in the hands of the God who will redeem it, or who already has.

If Christianity is true, God gives us good and only good: incredible richness of entity and function, incredible resources of matter and spirit, incredible freedom to determine how we shall use his gifts. In Boethius' words, "Every lot is good . . . whether be it harsh or be it pleasing." But we do not habitually see things in that way. We take the gifts as prerogatives and abuse them. We pervert the gift of diversity, which might extend immeasurably the range of our joy, and create from it the evil

171

of schism. We interpret the wholeness of integrity to mean homo-
geneity. Ill will, stupidity, and irresponsibility convert God's
good into our evil, until the fortunes of birth, living, and death
become harsh beyond any foreseeable redemption, and are clearly
beyond redemption by any human power. To such man-made
evils must be added those for which man has no apparent responsibility: the wonder of cell reproduction raging uncontrol-
lably in cancer; plagues and hurricanes; children born with
deformities of body and mind. Every lot is good — all luck is
good — in these?

To say with Boethius that "All luck is good" is not to offer
a description of events or things. It is to establish a particular
relation between the self and the world: the relation of hope.
The events and entities that we call evil are not only lacking
in good; many of them are positively evil. In hoping, we declare
our intention to seek even in them the God of whom it is
written that he is with those who make their bed in hell. We
do not understand why God permits evil. Neither do we understand why he permits what we call good. Yet we do not need
to understand in order to praise.

It is true that often praise is facilitated by intellectual apprehension of the good that an event contains. To conclude, however, that praise is possible only where we have definable reasons for praising is to neglect such phenomena as our impulsive,
unreasonable adoration of love, beauty, the shining goodness of
a face, the exquisitely detailed and precise obedience to law
manifested by a mountain stream, and other wonders we do not
at all understand. We can praise God with reasons and without
them; and we can praise him against reason — not by denying
the existence or validity of our contrary reasoning, but by affirming our determination that the contradictions shall themselves
become means of his grace.

Our terms are not God's terms. Our reasonable joy with good
cause is not his joy without a cause, and if we insist on having
our own joy on our own terms, we shall not have his. Humanly
speaking, "All luck is good" is sentimental nonsense of the most
vicious sort. It implies a disastrous, damnable blurring of the
difference between good and evil. Christianly speaking, it means
the resolve to hold fast to God though all the devils in hell
array themselves against us. Our hope is in the God who is
present with us whether we perceive him or not, and is never

closer to us than when we do not see him. By looking within the immediate, actual present events for the God who sustains us in them, we practice the virtue of hope.

Our evidence that he sustains us now does not come from our experience of life as harsh or pleasing, but from the straightforward, elemental fact that we are being sustained by something other than ourselves. The air we breathe, the food we eat, the ground we rest our weight on, have not been generated by our minds and wills. Our capacities to think and to love, our freedom to adore and resist, are bequeathed to us by powers outside ourselves. Our very limitations are gifts, although we may not welcome them or know what to do with them. We are children who have so set our hearts on one thing that we trample on the greater thing which we have received instead. Being denied the end we desire, we furiously repudiate the nobler end for which we were made. Refusing joy as a gift, we demand happiness as a right.

Earlier, I said that the easy answer to "Where is our hope?" is: "Our hope is in God." It needs now to be said that this is the Christian answer, although Christianly it is not easy, however glibly it falls from the lips of those who do not know what a terrible thing they are saying. If the God who permits this pain or that injustice or those catastrophes is both omnipotent and good, then goodness does not mean what we have taken it to mean, and the distinction between good and evil cannot be made on the easy basis that we thought it could. The Holy Spirit who is the Gift and Grace and Power of God is indeed abroad in the world, but what he gives is so unexpected that we deny him in his gifts. Again and again the Lord has appeared on our doorstep, and we have failed to recognize him because he was not wearing his robes of state.

Being in sin, we do not know what is good, and we can expect to be repelled by those things whose goodness extends deeper or higher or wider than we are currently able to comprehend. We can also expect that any progress we make toward clarifying our perception of the good will be laborious and painful. The Holy Spirit will appear to us more often as the skeleton at the feast than as its convivial host, because our eyes are not educated to pierce his different disguises. Our problem lies in learning to recognize the Person in all his functions and forms. He is wholly good, with so potent a goodness that he can embrace evil and redeem it, until in the end the cry which defined our relation to the world, "All luck is good," becomes his description of all that exists. Our hope for the future springs from our praise to the God of the present.

4. *The End of the World*

In 1963, I went back to Swarthmore for my twenty-fifth reunion. During the day and a half of that affair, I looked at the world with a kind of double vision and lived a double life. Myself-at-twenty was alive again in myself-at-forty-five, the one still tormented by her question, "Why live?", the other bearing an answer.

I did not bring myself-at-twenty the answer she was seeking: an authoritative or even a persuasive reason for living. All I could do was to show her whom she had become, in order for her to know that her agony had not been — was not to be — wasted. She had not been able to see her place in the pattern of my development or in any larger pattern that included us both, and myself-at-forty-five could see only as much of it as was already incarnate. But this much I could set before her in love and gratitude, to give her hope: that she and I had not created the pattern; we had discovered it.

My conviction that the process has been one of discovering — not of creating — a meaningful pattern is certainly the result of a decision so to believe, and I suppose the decision results as much from my astonishment with the pattern I now can see as from anything else. It seems that when I have sought and followed what rang true to me, the resulting order of events has been not only strikingly different from anything I had imagined, expected, desired, or planned, but also far more satisfying — although taking into account the pain and the sheer, dogged, monotonous work into which those bells have led me, I must add that in this context, satisfaction does not imply happiness. It means something closer to the strenuous meeting of a demand or realization of a possibility, in which every fibre of one's being is strained to the utmost.

To say that the pattern is discovered implies that it already exists, but it does not necessarily imply that my destiny was laid down for me by a blind fate or an all-seeing providence. It can equally well mean that I was created for a particular end whose nature does not depend upon my awareness or choice, and that the ringing true indicates my approach to the end I cannot envision. While that destiny may have been planned, it was not in any sense predetermined whether I should fulfil it or fall short or move into some completely different pattern, or succeed or fail at any specific point. Nothing has compelled me to incarnate the meaning that — I believe — was prepared for me from the beginning of the world, and within the fairly broad limits set by my heredity and environment, I could have incarnated almost any pattern I chose.

For the Christian, the critical issue is what kinds of persons are created by our acts of incarnation: persons who, when they come face to face with their Lord, will kneel in adoring wonder, or turn away from him in hatred. But note that I have used the passive voice: persons who "are created": the process works indirectly. Our effort is directed toward obedience, not to making ourselves one or another sort of person. Whatever our individual patterns are like, we do not know them until they have become incarnate. Then, knowing what we are, we can choose to continue in that way or to depart from it. Our knowing depends upon incarnation, which is to say on obedience, and that which — he whom — we obey, we shall know: our own whims, or some abstract ideal, or the God who created a carnal world and redeemed it by a work of incarnation.

The Christian doctrine of creation is a way of saying that in all his dealings with us, God takes the initiative. He began everything, and nothing can continue without his faithfulness in supporting it. The doctrine of his love is a way of saying that he is in communion with us even when we deny our communion with him. He wills our freedom even though we use it to forsake him, and even though he knows that we shall — knew that we should — forsake him. Again, our language obstructs our thought. To say of God that he knows what we did is identical with saying that he knows what we are doing, and both these statements are identical with the declaration that he knows what we shall do tomorrow or next year or whenever. He does not, however, know in advance what we shall do because in him there is no future and no past. In the eternal present where he is said to be, there is only essential act, its end co-inhering in its beginning and its beginning suffused with the glory of its end.

I believe in an eternity which is outside time but permeating it, because nothing else explains my sense that the past and the future are wholly real: that myself-at-sixteen-and-twenty in her outrage and questioning lives still, and that myself-at-death stands beside me now. More broadly, Augustine suffers and rejoices with me, and I with those of coming generations who similarly live from him; and my friend who lives at a great distance can pray for me the prayer I cannot pray for myself. The substantial reality of history is derived from its relation to a non-historical order of existence in which nothing that once has been or will ever be incarnate is subject to ultimate discarnation.

It is impossible for me to think of such a permanent state in terms of bodies as we know them. My friend lives far away and does not yet know that I need her prayers. Augustine's flesh long ago disintegrated. Every molecule of my own body has been replaced several times over since I dreamed my dream: nothing in it is the same except its continuity of structure. In history, discarnation is continuous and final. Everything that once existed is lost or destroyed or forgotten, and the future has no carnal historical existence at all. Yet I am increasingly sure that both incarnations and discarnations are stages of being, rather than ends of being or illusions. All that is, was, and will be incarnate in history is eternally incarnate, continuous in structure although presumably not in the material from which it is made, and existing either within the heart of time and space or infinitely beyond them, as the ground of being or as the context within which being occurs.

I am speaking here of a mystery, and I am about to speak of a greater one. It is often said that in the presence of mysteries we should silence our meddling thoughts and babbling tongues, because a mystery cannot be understood and if we could understand it, we would destroy its quality as mystery. Such statements, however, confuse the mysterious with the puzzling. When a puzzle is solved, its puzzling character evaporates. But when a mystery is illuminated, its wonder is enhanced. The brighter the light thrown upon a mystery by question or examination or exploration, the more brilliant the glory reflected back from it into our eyes.

We do not profane the holy by investigating it or by formulating tentative interpretations of it. "There is no humility in refraining from asking the questions," Charles Williams has written; "the humility consists in believing that there may be

an answer." Similarly, it is not arrogant to present one's understanding of time or life or death or the world; it would be arrogant to offer it as more or other than our own, which we set
forth as a means for opening our hearts and minds to the knowledge, love, and worship of God. Here, as always, I do not know,
but my ignorance is not going to prevent me from inquiring
into the mysteries, or from sharing whatever I find.

If history is real in an eternal sense that transcends its apparent reality, then death is a real outrage against incarnate
nature and eternal love. It is the supreme discarnation, the
shattering of the fundamental condition for man's and the
world's existence. If man is made to be the incarnation of
the Incarnate Lord, then in dying, his function and therefore
his identity are annihilated. If the doctrine of incarnation is
true, at death the spirit does not float loose from the confining
flesh: the two were one in life, and in death they share disintegration. But also, if incarnation is true, the dead are raised
from the dead. They do not rise by any power of their own,
but are raised from nothingness into perfect fulfilment. Their
incarnational nature is restored, and their reconciliation is
complete.

If incarnation is true...if. I cannot prove that it is; I can
only try to live with the doctrine, and in it. I am just beginning
to glimpse its implications: that my flesh does not war against
my spirit, although my bodily greeds and angers and prides
manifest impulses to evil in me which my fertile brain would
conceal if they showed themselves only in mental forms. My
spirit is not impatient for its release from nature, but is pressing
importunately toward that healing that results from integration
with it. Disease certainly is a sign of failure in reconciliation,
but it is the height of effrontery to blame ourselves for its inci-
dence or consequences. We belong to a natural order which we
did not create and can control only a little; to claim that by our
sin we bring disease upon ourselves is to claim a hegemony over
nature that challenges God's authority over us and his faithfulness to his creation. Apart from abusing our bodies by care-
lessness, self-will, and culpable negligence, any connection between disease and retribution for particular sins is fortuitous.

Those of us who are Christian can indeed properly blame
God for involving us in the sins of the whole world, but having
done so, we had better get to work using the world properly,

curing or enduring or enjoying or redeeming it as he permits, rather than postponing remedial action while we indulge ourselves in remorse. Repentance — turning hopefully to God — is never out of place, because it is the whole person who bears the illness and who is healed or dies. The restoration of the body is a blessing to the mind and heart, and the acts of bodily dissolution can be taken into God by his triumphant will. But the body is not so dependent upon the spirit that physical disease can always or often be attributed to the sins of the spirit, or healed by the forgiveness of sins.

The reconciliation for which we hope is taking place daily within and among ourselves, if we do not refuse it. The resurrection from the dead is only one of its forms, and what we believe concerning resurrection will depend in great part upon what we have known of these other forms. Our hope for the integration of death with life in resurrection springs out of the integrations that have already been achieved in us. Because we have died time and again in small ways, and have been raised time and time again out of the wreckage, we expect that the final resurrection will be preceded by a final death. As we have feared and hated and resisted our small deaths, we can expect to fear and hate and resist our final death with a final energy worthy of the occasion. So be it. We shall not need to save our energy for rising from the dead, if our past and present experiences are faithful guides. We shall not rise; we shall be raised. We do not live forever; we die and are reborn.

Again, we cannot prove that this is true. We can only live with and in it. What will happen when we live in it, no man knows in advance, and if God knows, it is because he sees all things as we see the history behind ourselves and as we shall see them in eternity. He knows our ends because in him they are already accomplished. He does not determine what we are going to do — even within time, neither he nor we cause things to happen simply by knowing that they have happened or are happening or will happen. He does not foresee how we are going to die: in him we have already died. He does not intend to raise us from the dead at some future time: he is raising us now.

Myself-at-twenty had been all but overwhelmed by the fear without a cause. In myself-at-forty-five, that fear had been healed by the Person of Joy in his gift of the joy without a cause. We are reconciled, she and I, because we are both in him, and such is his nature that he loves us whether we are lovable or not, without stint or hesitation or qualification. The reconciliation had always existed, although it took me a quarter of a century to find it. During part of that time, I had been satisfied that God exists, and this indeed was a cause for joy. But we can know the causes of things without joining in the proceedings. We can know who God is without meeting him. Or we can meet him without knowing who he is. Yet he knows us, and we live under the promise — or the threat — that he will identify himself to us. Then we shall know ourselves as we are known by him: as creatures who were made for joy, and who are accepting or refusing his joy. Now we are living eternally in him, or dying eternally in ourselves.

5. *The Given Name*

According to traditional Christian doctrine, Jesus the Christ is not merely the embodiment of reconciliation; it is his gift. He does not merely reveal the way, the truth, and the life; they are his manner of relating himself to us, and we know them when we know ourselves in him. Out of the exchanges of knowing and being known, loving and being loved, spring the doctrines and definitions which — Christians say — are valid expressions of the truth which is constituted by the relationship itself.

The absolute priority of the relationship over its formulation in dogma is superbly expressed by the fact that in the Hebrew-Christian tradition, God is not defined: he is named. He is not postulated: he is met. He is not identified by qualities or functions, but by reference to persons: "the God of Abraham, Isaac, and Jacob," "the God and Father of our Lord Jesus Christ." The pivot of the entire Old Testament is the command, "Thou shalt have no other gods before Me"; the pivot of the New is, "Thou shalt love the Lord thy God with all thy heart, and with all thy soul, and with all thy strength, and with all thy mind." The Old Testament speaks of the relation between God and man in terms of a covenant, the New in terms of love. Both specify that it is a relation of persons.

A personal relation is by its nature reciprocal. The persons know and are known by one another. When the Hebrew and the Christian speak of knowing God, they are committing themselves to the affirmation that God knows them. Each with his own voice names God, and God names each of them. They can name him because he has already named them: it was he who made them capable of responding personally to him. The essential requirement for Hebrew and Christian alike is to enter and sustain the reciprocal relation between himself and God.

Reciprocity involves a tension, an energy, which must be unceasingly protected against our natural tendencies to seek a static equilibrium. We are offered a dynamic balance like that of a living body; we prefer the static balance of a stone. We are more comfortable in obeying fixed rules that we can exactly define than in co-ordinating our activities with those of other persons, human or divine. Naturally, therefore, we tend to modify the central demand of the Christian faith that God only is to be our God, by yoking the one command with other commands, and identifying other things with him. In the Old Testament, it is recorded that some people wanted both God and nature gods; later some predicated a God who ruled Israel and other gods of Israel's enemies. In Christian history there have been the first century Judaizers — God and the Law of Moses; the opponents of Copernicus and Galileo — God and Ptolemaic astronomy; the enemies of Darwin — God and the doctrine of special creation; the moralists — God and right conduct; the ecclesiastics — God and the church; the emotionalists — God and certain feelings or moods; and so on down the line.

None of these combinations has been officially promulgated to any extent as an alternative to God alone, but all have been widely employed as equivalents to him — for example, in "If you are in right relation to God, you will conform to the definition of right behavior that we give you," or, "If you are not a member of a church, it means that you are not in right relation to God." The step is scarcely perceptible from such "God and" statements to the substitution of an ethical norm or church membership for obedience to God. We are continually being tempted away from God into the innumerable varieties of God and something simpler to comprehend, easier to do, and more comfortable to live with.

Such evasions of the two first commandments, the Old and the New, are apparent not only when we lapse into "God and" attitudes, binding him to a theology or creed or ideal or institution or priest or prophet, but also when we bind ourselves in obedience to something other than him. The self has only two options: to be authentically itself and not some other thing, or to be some other thing, a counterfeit self. Either we answer when God speaks our name, or we answer to the names we choose for ourselves and each other. For years I called myself "Wife" and found that I could not be a satisfactory wife until I became "Me". I wanted my name to be "Mother", and found that I could not hear God's name for me until I had relinquished the name I had given to myself. Time after time, others have insisted that my name was or ought to be Christian, Liberal, Mature, Socially Adjusted, and I was reproved so severely for questioning those identifications that blaming myself for recalcitrance, I pretended that such names were really mine until the lie sickened me. For years I heard my own name in the bells that rang true to me, without knowing whose voice spoke through the bells. I still do not hear it very clearly, but I hear it quite well enough to know that when I speak God's name, I hear my own; that when I speak the name that is authentically my own, I hear his; and in that reciprocal interplay of naming, I learn the real names of his other creatures, and they learn mine.

To each of us God gives a different name and speaks a different word. With each of us he has a separate covenant, and from each of us he calls forth an individual response. Therefore it is only secondarily important for myself or anyone else to determine where I shall stand on ultimate issues, but it is overwhelmingly important to know with whom I take my stand, whose household of faith I shall choose to enter, which master I shall serve. In one sense I have no choice or initiative: he who knows my real name is my master, even though I rebel against his authority, because his name for me is the expression of my own nature and I cannot in the end escape myself. In another sense, the choice and initiative are, wholly mine. I can affirm my authentic nature and realize it — make it real — by incarnating it, or I can cease to be myself and become a non-entity, an illusion, fit for nothing except to be extinguished.

My name is the manifestation of my meaning. Therefore, as I see it now, the final answer to my original question, "Why live?", is the utterance of my name, and the answer to the question, "What does life mean?", is the utterance of God's name. In a most profound degree, the meaning of life is contained in the simple declaration, "I know you," which God speaks to us and we to him. Life has meaning not because it is good or happy, but because it is created. The reason for living does not lie in a rational principle or a reasonable anticipation, but in the act of speaking to the God who has a name.

Among Christians, persons receive their names as the gift of the Holy Spirit in the sacrament of baptism. I have spent most of my life in learning that I was baptized — in discovering that I have a name which was given to me in the name of God and by God.

The greatest wonder of knowing that I am named, and in naming God with my own voice, is that by the power of that reciprocal act, I am brought into communion with all those who in his name give and receive their names. We form one of the households of the Faith, knowing and being known by one another because we *name* our Lord. Therefore our unity is grounded in the Old and New Writings, and our rule is the discipline of readiness to hear the one Name and to speak all names. So doing, we ratify one another and ourselves as created beings, and we incarnate — each in his own style and degree — the primal joy of creation when the morning stars are said to have sung together. The community of the named is not merely a future possibility to which we look forward with the emotion of hope: it is a present reality in which we participate by the virtue of hope, and being incarnate, it is eternally real.

* * * * * *

The ending of this account marks the conclusion of a stage in my theological development, not the completion of my theology. What I have written here is explicitly and deliberately an interim report, and I do not expect to write a final one. As it stands now, my theology is badly unbalanced, having much too little weight on man as a social being and on social structures and functions. And it is seriously incomplete, especially in its Christology. I am not especially worried about either of these defects, or any others. For one thing, I am not — at this point — trying to answer all my questions or to solve all human problems or to provide a generally comprehensive system. For another, I fully expect that in his own time and way, God will see to it that my insufficiencies and errors are corrected, as he has already seen to it that my over-emphasis on the Way of the

Rejection of Images should be corrected by the movement currently taking place toward the Way of their Affirmation.

Indeed, by the time the second draft of this book was finished, I found myself being thrust into activities whose influence is already threatening certain parts of my theology. It seems as if the God who once led me out of the Church and the City and into the wilderness is now leading me back into them. That is emphatically not a direction I want to go, but having resisted it vigorously for some time, I have begun to suspect that here is another battle that I must fight to the death and shall lose.

Contemplating my involvement in the Church and the City, I find myself looking not only forward but back, and what strikes me most forcibly in the landscape is its absurdity. All those terrible struggles have been to obtain the joy that has always lain in my own hands, to see the world in which I have lived all my life, to hear the bells that have resounded in my ears since my baptism. My theologizing has been deadly serious, but I see it now as the seriousness of playing a game — a game not of make-believe, but of the poet who disciplines his thought into an appropriate form, of the explorers who climb mountains because they are there, of children darting back and forth on the shore of the sea, chasing and being chased by the waves.

If I had not been torn and broken in the game, I might not have become capable of joy. All is gift, even the power to receive the gift, but the willingness to receive and the arts of receiving have not come easily to me. No doubt most of my hells have been of my own creation, but I am not ready to declare that they were unnecessary, much less unreal. It seems that I had to incarnate those hells before I could offer them for redemption, and sometimes I had to incarnate them in order to identify them as hells. The process is still going on. I am certain that other hells lie before me, and that they cannot be conquered until I have inhabited and recognized and repudiated them. But all has been well, all shall be well, and all is well. From the far reaches of the eternal present, I occasionally hear the infinitely tender, infinitely joyous sound of God laughing at me in love, and sometimes I can laugh with him.

"To me also was given, if not Victory, yet the consciousness of Battle, and the resolve to persevere therein while life or faculty is left." I do not know what the end is, or why I was given the consciousness of battle, or where I shall go from here. I am not sure that in the end there will be anything to say for me except that I have not refused the battle. Yet I am resolved to persevere therein, and in that resolution I offer the battle to the Lord who gave it to me, in gratitude and praise for his gift.

EPILOGUE

Never did He make two things the same; never did He utter one word twice. After earths, not better earths but beasts; after beasts, not better beasts but spirits. After a falling, not recovery but a new creation. Out of the new creation, not a third but the mode of change itself is changed forever.

C. S. Lewis, *Perelandra*

chapter eight

DOING IT YOURSELF IN THEOLOGY

Not only then has each man his individual relation to God, but each man has his peculiar relation to God. He is to God a peculiar being, made after his own fashion, and that of no one else; . . . hence he can worship God as no man else can worship him, — can understand God as no man else can understand him.

GEORGE MACDONALD, *Unspoken Sermons*, Series I

Now, my dear reader, it is your turn. I have shown you the development of my theology in order to illustrate the process, to suggest standards of adequacy and authenticity, and to encourage you to try your own hand at theologizing. If you merely acquiesce in or debate my conclusions, the book will not have been worth my writing or your reading.

If you are fortunate enough to have direct and competent guidance by a teacher in your theological journey, you will not need any further word from me. If you do not, I have a special word of warning, and four words of counsel.

The word of warning has to do with the participation of others in developing and testing your own theology. You can no more theologize in isolation than you can live in isolation, and your greatest help and most disastrous obstructions will probably come from others. No one, by himself, can even guess at the magnificent range of ideas, interpretations, and systems that men through the ages have created and discovered, and that are available to stimulate and correct the beginner. No one can check his own thinking without reference to the thinking of others. These points should be so obvious as not to need further elaboration. Some of us, however, are occasionally tempted by our pride to see what we can do all by ourselves, a procedure which almost invariably results in merely repeating the blunders of the past rather than achieving fresh insights.

Less obvious in advance is the quantity and ferocity of the pressure that will probably be applied to you by any of your associates who knows of your interest in theology. The well-meaning will urge you to adopt their positions long before you are ready to take any stand. They will beseech you importunately to leave your own path and take theirs. Subtly, persistently, tyrannically, they will insist that you begin where they began, proceed according to their methods, and end at the place they have currently reached. If you are moving within the framework of Christianity, you will almost certainly be roundly criticized for preferring one mode or degree of incarnation — as in the sacraments — over another, and admonished in and out of season for trying to think these matters through instead of meekly swallowing the judgments of some professional theologian. And you can expect that nearly everyone — except the professionals themselves — will be impatient to tell you which theologian you should defer to.

Listen to all these people, at least in the beginning. You will need all the help you can get, and here is one of the places where help is most readily available. But do not give your loyalty, or even your consent, too soon. It will take time and careful thought for you to select from among the conflicting demands those to which you should pay further attention. It is fairly important that you select rightly, but with rare exceptions it is infinitely more important that you select wisely. That is, the standards by which you make your selection are more crucial than the discrete ideas or courses of action which result from applying those standards. For example, you will need to know whether on a particular issue you are choosing on the basis of preference, or of such a principle as rational coherence or reasonable integrity, and if a principle, what one or ones and how they are related to one another, or if a preference, what kind of person is reflected and created by yielding to that preference. Neither principles nor preferences are good in themselves, and a large part of your theological task will be to determine and test your standards.

At the outset, you may find it useful to adopt another's standards as a working hypothesis, as I took mine more or less directly from philosophy and psychology. Presumably you will modify or completely change them as you go further, so that they will more adequately apply to your particular situation and needs. No two theologians have quite the same standards because they do not use quite the same materials. We differ in our resources and experiences, our problems and limitations. Therefore theologies that are exactly alike are as suspect as identical examination papers. However, we share a common humanity and, through conversation and reading, a common knowledge about many matters. Therefore our theologies should have certain similarities, and we can learn from one another even though we cannot duplicate one another.

If your theology conforms too closely with that of another person, it is likely that you have not absorbed his ideas fully into yourself. If it is too peculiarly your own, presumably you are in danger of being cut off from the process of living interchange which is the ultimate source of theology. In both cases, what constitutes "too much" or "too little" will be determined by your individual balance, which in turn is to be judged on the basis of general direction of movement rather than of momentary states. A theology, like a person, does not grow at the same rate on all levels or in all directions.

Every theology is the expression of the manner in which a unique individual has involved himself in the life of his time. A theology may be wide in scope, representing a manner of involvement which a great many people have employed during many times. Or it may be limited to a few people or only one: I think of the radically individualistic theology of William Blake. The manner of involvement, however, consists of a series of historical events and is therefore susceptible to an indefinite number of interpretations, while the theology is the declaration of a particular interpretation. Thus the incidents in my life can be taken as meaning something entirely different from the interpretations I have assigned to them. A secular humanist could very well conclude from this report that the human capacity for self-deception has even more vagaries than he had hitherto suspected, or a psychologist might consider it a type case of a certain variety of pathological aberration.

Theologizing as a conscious process cannot "begin at the beginning and go on till you come to the end; then stop." It can only begin in the middle. We must start where we are with the loosely or tightly organized ideas of the world and ourselves that we have been accumulating since our birth if not before, and the roughly satisfactory patterns of expectation and response that we have lived with for many years. We cannot live without at least a vaguely coordinated assortment of attitudes, a kind of proto-theology which will become a theology when it is formulated. We must have an integration of sorts before we can begin theologizing, and this will determine our individual points of departure.

Often, perhaps always, our journey is motivated by a breakdown in our proto-theology. Our old system disintegrates or we see that it was never satisfactorily inclusive, and rather than live in chaos, we seek a new pattern. Specific advice on how or in what direction to proceed can be given only for specific situations, and no advice at all can be given except from the standpoint of a specific theology. The suggestions that follow, therefore, are not to be construed as universally valid rules for theologizing, but only as the sharing of a limited and only partially digested experience.

Use your common sense. Work at your own level and pace. If you have access to competent professional instruction and the time, money, and inclination to take advantage of it, by all means do so. If not, search in books and conversation until you find someone who speaks to your condition in your own language, and follow where he leads, being careful to take account of what his critics have said about him. Assuming that you care enough about the enterprise to think and not just coddle your prejudices, you need not worry about remaining on the level where you began. As your capacity to handle the material increases, you will be less content with what you have on hand, and will move on at the first promising opportunity. And with practice, your ability to discriminate between promising and unpromising opportunities will grow.

But do not hurry and do not let yourself be hurried. We are not required by common sense either to rush or to dally, but rather to adjust our speed to our circumstances. Where the road lies clear before us, we can move swiftly. Where we do not know what to do next, we can usually wait for a little while to study the maps or discuss the options with our companions, or, if nothing else, we can proceed circumspectly. Two of the major temptations along the way are that we shall stop too soon, making our home in some village only part way to Jerusalem, and that we shall recklessly accelerate so that we lose our way entirely or destroy ourselves and others in collisions. A speed that is safe for a professional theologian may be exceedingly dangerous for an apprentice who is working alone. However, unless the apprentice takes advantage of his opportunities to move swiftly, he will never learn to do more than crawl at his job.

By the same token, do not try to impose your speed on others. Share what you have. Challenge, stimulate, criticize, argue, describe, and whenever necessary ask for explanations in terms that you can understand. But do not insist or demand. Do not use your strength to drive another faster than he is ready to move, or your weakness to hold him back. For the last time, "Let no man be hasty to eat of the fruits of paradise before his time"; but also, let not man be impatient with others or permit his own patience to degenerate into sloth.

Common sense also requires that we not lose sight of the simple, the obvious, the immediate, and the direct. Most of us have been exhaustively trained to look beneath the surface of things, on the ground that appearances are deceptive — and so they often are. We can, however, admit that the superficial aspects of an event or person do not give us the whole picture, without denying that they give us a part of the picture and often a critically important part. It is sometimes the perceived surface, not the presumed depth, which exhibits the clue to truth. Quite often we do mean exactly what we say, and so do others: our words are not always contrary to our intentions and motives, and our actions reveal at least as much as they conceal of the person who acts. The ingenious interpreter who takes nothing at face value will discern the inconsequential symptom that he wants to find more often than the palpable signal that is there.

The mood of our time is cynical rather than skeptical. We have enthroned the anti-hero and cut the saint down to our own size. We despise beauty in literature and art, and scoff at honor

191

and dignity. So doing, we have entangled ourselves in the net of our own cleverness. But the perception of the cynic is no more accurate than the perception of the sentimentalist, and they are equally far from the sanity of common sense and of the wisdom into which it flowers.

Be responsible. We may be working alone — there are times when we must work alone — but we are not living alone. The whole social fabric and every person in it — present, future, and past — depends upon what each of us does and leaves undone. Our entire lives — now, tomorrow, and yesterday — depend upon what every other person does and leaves undone. Social and individual responsibility is therefore not only a duty for the citizen but an imperative for the theologian in his dealings with both persons and ideas.

An especially important form of theological responsibility is the requirement that he be accurate. For example, nearly everyone who is at all acquainted with Christianity believes himself to be an authority on it, quite without respect to his theological and historical study of the subject, church membership, or experience with a wide range of persons who call themselves Christian. Historically and theologically, Christianity can be identified, although it is as difficult as describing a person verbally in contrast to pointing him out or exhibiting a picture of him. But both the proponents and the opponents of the Christian faith, not to mention the indifferent, seem to exult in representing it inaccurately, setting their straw men on a pedestal or hanging them from the nearest tree.

To narrow the illustration: properly understood, Christianity does not have or pretend to have all the answers, if only because it is not concerned with all the questions. Within the realm of religious questions, some of its answers are less attractive than those of certain non-Christian religions. Thus in answer to the query, "How can we escape from pain?", it replies, "Under God in Christ, we cannot." Yet there are many who interpret Christianity incorrectly, imprecisely, and treacherously in order to avoid such distasteful answers. There are excellent grounds for attacking and defending Christianity and every other major religion, and it is incumbent even upon the novice in theology that he be scrupulously just in dealing with them all.

As theologians, lay or professional, we are constantly working with great ideas whose power to create or destroy can sweep us off our feet, and great problems that can throw us into abysses of confusion or maelstroms of exaltation. Any idea or virtue or course of action, even the truest or holiest, becomes error or sin if it is carried to an extreme. Justice untempered by love, love untempered by reason, reason untempered by skepticism, skepticism untempered by faith — their destructiveness is readily apparent. We restrain our temptation toward the over-simplifications of fanaticism by becoming both sympathetic and critical, neither swallowing ideas whole nor spitting them out before we have savored them. Successively or simultaneously as the particular balance and integration of our minds will determine, we need to understand them as if from within and to evaluate them as if from outside.

Neither a balanced nor an integrated person is necessarily in equilibrium at every moment. One can properly concentrate for hours or years on a single problem, or be caught for months in one stage of stress. Like Kierkegaard and many others, one may take and hold for a long period a position which is in itself unbalanced in order to counteract another extreme in the world to which he is speaking. In a society ridden with conformism, an exaggerated individualism may represent a true balance between the theologian and the community. Among radical nonconformists, one may have to over-emphasize the function of the community in order to be heard at all.

No form of inaccuracy is more serious than that in which the eccentricities of our own local circumstances are taken to be universal characteristics of society and persons, or the flaming issues of our short generation taken as perennial controversies. Some areas where we see no room for argument were once centers of vehement debate; some of our most acute disturbances occur in realms where earlier generations found no problems at all. Certainly the very great, very general questions seem always to have been asked: What is man? What is the world? What can we know? What should we do? Even so, they are differently stressed in different eras and regions. Rarely if ever in the history of thought has the nature of man been so passionately argued as it is today, but we err if we interpret the philosophers and theologians of the past as if they were equally wrapped up in the same problem. Likewise, we err if we fail to grasp the significance of their problems because we are so narrowly focussed on our own.

Discipline yourself, but be sure that the disciplines you undertake are right for you. Every science and art, occupation and vocation, has its own techniques and procedures and its own standards of adequacy. The disciplines of patience and fairmindedness are prerequisites for competence in nearly every field; so are persistence and willingness to learn. The specific techniques that the theologian needs to master will depend upon whether his bent is toward analysis or synthesis or practical action or contemplation, and whether he understands theology to be primarily a science, an art, a guide for living, a complement to worship, or a combination of these or others. At various times and in the persons of various theologians, Christian theology has performed all those functions, and the Christian lay theologian, as part of his discipline, should be at least acquainted with them all, even though he may be actively engaged in only one or two phases of the total enterprise.

There is no virtue in any theological or religious disciplines for their own sakes. They are means for tempering the metal of our intellects and spirits. Here the lay theologian is likely to be substantially handicapped, because whatever the degree of his self-discipline, he needs also the discipline of external criticism and guidance, which may be difficult to obtain and even more difficult to utilize. The professional, throughout his apprenticeship, benefited incalculably from measuring his thought against that of his superiors and peers. As journeyman and master, he has continued to present his work for appraisal by other theologians, who are usually swift and incisive in censuring obscurities, internal contradictions, omissions, and every other sin of sloppy or vacuous thinking, while they reinforce his commitment to the theological community and the goals and standards of theology.

Those of us who lack such high quality resistance and support must therefore guard ourselves with extraordinary diligence against whatever temptations beset us. They can seldom be identified in general: an ambiguity that is a fault in language analysis can be a virtue in a work of art; the fastidious attention to coherence that marks certain completed systems can be fatal in the early stages of creative thinking. We must learn for ourselves, and often by ourselves, not only how to resist temptation, but also how to differentiate between tendencies that are natural and right for us, and those that for us are unnatural or wrong. Indiscipline and improper discipline are equally disabling.

I do not know of any way by which the individual who is working by himself can discover and apply appropriate disciplines, except by wide and observant reading that is as much appreciative as captious — and not only reading in theology. For developing sensitivity to the structure of assumptions that underlies a world view, a novel is sometimes more effective than a textbook. For learning to identify consecutive and broken chains of reasoning, poetry can be more instructive than prose in openly displaying some types of coupling. For acquiring standards of precision there may be no better training than study of the great theologians, but in order to be precise they tend to hedge and qualify their statements so intricately that standards of clarity can usually be better learned through study of literature or by writing.

The layman usually cannot undertake a systematic review of the history of theology, and only occasionally is such a background either necessary or particularly desirable for his purposes — which are not altogether the same as the purposes of the professional. As lay theologians, we are not city planners or landscape architects or botanists or agronomists: we cultivate our gardens. It is an honorable task, and by no means easy. Some have said that technical theology is justified by its effect on our little gardens. It has also been said, though less often, that the fruits of our gardening are occasionally useful to professional scholars and teachers. We may not be able to breed new varieties of plants or perform chemical analysis of soils, but we can be diligent and skillful with spade, hoe, and pruning shears. We shall probably not grow food for the world in our little backyard plots of ground, but we can reasonably expect enough grapes for a few bottles of wine that we can share with our friends, and wheat for a few loaves of bread. As lay theologians, our primary job is in our own gardens; and our primary discipline is to live within our limitations and grow into our possibilities.

Hang on and keep going. Great problems call for great answers, and it takes patience, endurance, and courage to grow into the problems, much more into the answers. Courage is the one quality that is basic for any life that transcends mere biological existence. The word itself means more than confidence or bravery or fortitude, although it includes them all: it comes from the Latin word for heart, so that to be courageous is to have a heart, a vital center, an intrinsic life. Like all the other virtues, courage can be expressed in different styles: boldly in flamboyant acts of valor or shyly in unpretentious fortitude, gaily or sullenly, prudently or rashly. It is compatible with fear and indecision: one can be afraid and doubtful, yet forge ahead, or he can suspend his judgment when the courage to wait taxes his deepest reserves of strength. Courage can be properly or improperly directed, as implied in the phrase, "to have his heart in the right place"; it can be lacking, as in "he has lost heart."

Although courage can be deliberately cultivated, it is so difficult to generate or restore courage where it is entirely absent that the wisest are dismayed at the task. A temporary disheartenment can afflict the most courageous, but what of those who have lost all heart, who do not have the courage to face the act of choosing or the consequences of any choice? This is not a problem that I can answer in principle or handle in practice, but I have seen it often enough that I cannot brush it aside as a rare or minor disease. My present thinking about it is directed toward the relation between courage and integrity. I suspect that fundamentally, the lack of courage is a symptom of disintegrity, and disintegrity in whatever degree destroys courage in like degree. Similarly, excessive courage — courage not disciplined by responsibility and common sense — seems to be the result of a harshly inflexible or cramped integration. To force an integration, however, by laying violent hands upon oneself or others will also produce disintegration. When one part of the self dominates another by fiat, the person is divided against himself and in some sense his heart is broken.

Failures of courage lie at the roots of epidemic conformity and doctrinaire nonconformity alike: we permit our integrities to be fashioned in terms of others' integrities by submitting to or rebelling against theirs. Every person has his own style of integrity, his own manner of uniting his temperament, experiences, and reflections into a coordinated whole, and his own way of responding to the call of his Lord. At best it is not easy for most of us to discover our own styles, and when we do, we tend to universalize them. It is hard enough to be ourselves, God knows. It is harder still to free others, particularly those we love, to find their own integrities in their own times, their own ways, and to their own ends. It requires the great courage of great integrity to think clearly and to live in love, and so far as I know, there are no rules upon which we can surely depend, and only one guide — which is not very helpful in concrete situations. He who loves because he knows himself to be loved will be less apt to err than he who loves in order to obtain love. He who has received his integrity as a gift from God will not be prone to overbear the integrities that God has given to others.

The courage to keep going, to refuse premature solutions, to wait in darkness, to reject what does not ring true: these only hint at the forms of courage which are needed for living, and therefore for theologizing. In addition, there is one other which may be the most important of all: the courage to make mistakes. Few terrors are as disabling as the fear of being wrong; consequently, our sins from timidity frequently outweigh our sins from boldness. Because we are finite and sinful, we are wrong whatever we do. But also, if we do nothing we are wrong, and what we do may very well be right. Therefore it behooves us to walk humbly on our journey, but also to walk bravely.

Common sense. Social responsibility. Discipline. Courage. The exercise of these qualities — which are the cardinal virtues of both classical and Christian tradition: prudence, justice, temperance (as steel is tempered), and fortitude — will not guarantee that we shall know the truth and attain integrity within the truth. They are means for growing and defenses against the most vicious enemies of growth: unreality, isolation, fragmentation, and despair. And they are preparatory exercises for developing the virtues that traditional Christianity has said are the highest of all: faith, hope, and love.

The cardinal virtues carry no inviolable promise. Nothing that we can do, however, does carry such a guarantee. We cannot bargain with life, much less with God — at least, not with the Christian God. We can plant the seed, but it is he who gives or does not give the increase, and often the one who reaps is not the one who had sown. The covenant that we make with him by responding to his covenant with us is not a treaty or a pledge, but a decision to respond to Love with love. It is the choice to live by incarnating love whatever the situation and consequences, and we are not told in advance what the consequences will be.

One final word: as lay theologians, we stand within the company of those who in all ages have faced the same problems and fought the same battles. We can read among them to find our companions when we grow lonely. Their solutions may not answer our specific questions, but in their certainty that an answer can be found, we gain new heart for hanging on and new boldness in pressing forward. In sharing their triumphs, we receive a sign of our own. It does not matter that we are novices among the masters of theology. If we care enough about the great problems of living to work at them, we belong to the company of theologians and they are working with us, as we with them.

"Ask and you shall receive" — and in the receiving, you will finally discover what it was you had asked for. "Seek and you shall find" — and what you find will reveal the nature and meaning of your search. "Knock and the door will be opened unto you" — so take heed in choosing among the doors you face. Do not ask for anything less than fullness of life, or seek anything smaller than truth, or knock at any door that is too low or narrow for you to enter when you stand at your full height. Fight the good fight; finish the course; keep the faith.

A LIST OF BOOKS

...and articles, including fiction, non-fiction, and poetry, which at one time or another have particularly nourished or stimulated or enlightened me on my theological journey.

Margery Allingham. *The China Governess.* New York: Doubleday, 1962. Fiction.

———. *The Tiger in the Smoke.* London: Chatto & Windus, 1952. Fiction.

J. Redwood Anderson. *Transvaluations.* London: Oxford University Press, 1932. Poetry.

Charlotte Armstrong. *A Dram of Poison.* New York: Coward-McCann, 1956. Fiction.

G. K. Chesterton. *The Ballad of the White Horse.* London: Methuen, 1927 (9th edition). Poetry.

———. *The Man Who Was Thursday.* New York: Boni, 1908. Fiction.

———. *Orthodoxy.* New York: J. Lane, 1909. Non-fiction.

Trygve Gulbranssen. *Beyond Sing the Woods.* New York: Putnam, 1936. Fiction.

Dag Hammarskjöld. *Markings.* New York: Knopf, 1964. Non-fiction.

Katharine Butler Hathaway. *The Little Locksmith.* New York: Coward-McCann, 1943. Non-fiction.

Nikos Kazantzakis. *Report to Greco.* New York: Simon & Schuster, 1965. Non-fiction.

Walter Kerr. *The Decline of Pleasure.* New York: Simon & Schuster, 1965. Non-fiction.

Laurence Lafore. *Learner's Permit.* New York: Doubleday & Co., 1962. Fiction.

C. S. Lewis. Most of his published work, but especially:

———. *The Discarded Image.* Cambridge: The University Press, 1964. Non-fiction.

———. *An Experiment in Criticism.* Cambridge: The University Press, 1961. Non-fiction.

———. *The Great Divorce.* New York: Macmillan, 1959. Fiction.

———. *A Grief Observed.* London: Faber & Faber, 1964. Non-fiction.

———. *Surprised by Joy.* New York: Harcourt Brace, 1956. Non-fiction.

John Livingston Lowes. *The Road to Xanadu.* Boston: Houghton Mifflin, 1927. Non-fiction.

George Macdonald. *Unspoken Sermons, First Series.* London: Alexander Strahan, 1867. Non-fiction.

John Macmurray. *The Self as Agent* and *Persons in Relation* (Gifford Lectures, 1953-1954). New York: Harper & Row, 1957 and 1961. Non-fiction.

A List of Books

Charlotte Mew. *Collected Poems*. London: G. Duckworth, 1953. Poetry.

Charles Morgan. Most of his published work, but especially:

———. *The Fountain*. London: Macmillan, 1932. Fiction.

———. Preface to *The Flashing Stream*. London: Macmillan, 1938. Non-fiction.

———. *Selected Letters*, edited by Eilunid Lewis. London: Macmillan, 1967. Non-fiction.

———. *Sparkenbroke*. London: Macmillan, 1936. Fiction.

———. *The Voyage*. London: Macmillan, 1940. Fiction.

———. *The Writer and His World*. London: Macmillan, 1960. Non-fiction.

Lewis Mumford. "The Revolt of the Demons." *The New Yorker*, May 23, 1964, pp. 155-185. Non-fiction.

Romain Rolland. *Jean-Christophe*. New York: Holt, 1910-1911.

Dorothy L. Sayers. Most of her published work, but especially:

———. *Busman's Honeymoon*. New York: Harcourt, Brace, 1937. Fiction.

———. *Creed or Chaos*. London: Methuen, 1947. Non-fiction.

———. *Gaudy Night*. New York: Harcourt, Brace, 1936. Fiction.

———. *The Mind of the Maker*. London: Methuen, 1941. Non-fiction.

John V. Taylor. *The Primal Vision*. Philadelphia: Fortress Press, 1964. Non-fiction.

J. R. R. Tolkien. *The Lord of the Rings*. A Trilogy. Boston: Houghton Mifflin, 1954-1956. Fiction.

———. "On Fairy Tales." In *Essays Presented to Charles Williams*. Grand Rapids: Wm. B. Eerdmans, 1966. Non-fiction.

Vercors. *You Shall Know Them*. New York: Little, Brown, 1953. Fiction. (Also published under the author's own name and with another title: Jean Bruller. *The Murder of the Missing Link*. New York: Pocket Books, 1955.)

Helen C. White. *A Watch in the Night*. New York: Macmillan, 1935. Fiction.

Charles Williams. Most of his published work, but especially:

———. *Descent into Hell*. Grand Rapids: Wm. B. Eerdmans, 1965. Fiction.

———. *The Figure of Beatrice*. London: Faber & Faber, 1943. Non-fiction.

———. *He Came Down from Heaven* (including *The Forgiveness of Sins*). London: Faber & Faber, 1950. Non-fiction.

———. *The Image of the City and Other Essays*, edited by Anne Ridler. London: Oxford University Press, 1958. Non-fiction.

Austin Tappan Wright. *Islandia*. New York: Farrar & Rinehart, 1942. Fiction.